Siren Songs
Seven Stories Applied to Marriage

Doug & Mirjam

May God bless and confirm you always.

With sincere appreciation.

We love you guys.

Dane & Naomi Ville

June 2018

Siren Songs
Seven Stories Applied to Marriage

Dr. Daniel Villa

Siren Songs, seven stories applied to marriage.
© 2015 Dr. Daniel Villa

Contact the Author:
Dr. Daniel Villa
Email: dnvilla99@gmail.com
www.impactofamiliar.com

Originally Published in Spanish under the title:
Cantos de Sirena, siete relatos aplicados al matrimonio.

English Translation by James McKerihan

Cover Design: Ronald Solis
Illustrations: Junior Sanchez

ISBN: 978-0-9758966-2-4

Category: Married Life

Printed in the United States of America

Dedication

To my wife Naíme, my companion and friend.
To my children Jessica, Lisset, Patricia,
Dan, Alex and Raúl.
To my parents Ramón Villa and Gladys Ventura,
and to my beloved siblings.

Special Recognition

To my wife Naíme for her patience and help
with the selection of the material for the book.
To Rev. James McKerihan for the English Translation.
To Ivannia Pérez and Yohana De Los Santos
for their help in editing and revision.
To Ronald Solís for his hard work on the cover,
and to Junior Sánchez for the illustrations.

Index

Prologue

Our society suffers from an endemic illness that is attacking the fibers of the structure that sustains it. As happens in all immunological diseases, this scourge attacks with the purpose of dismantling the immune system that protects the entire organism. We are talking about the family, traditionally known as the mainstay of society, and in particular, its fundamental principle: the institution of marriage. Referring to marriage, the great Socrates said to one of his disciples: "Get married. If you find a good woman, you will be happy; if not, you will become a philosopher." Although this is a common joke, the perspective of the philosopher is not necessary to have a good marriage. Nonetheless, the "apparently" better married couples today seem to have adopted it as a rule and basic principle for maintaining their home life.

To counteract this evil so widespread all over the world, many books have been written. So much so that one of the important sections in any bookstore deals with the topic of marriage. Even more so now, in our cybernetic world with its exceedingly varied works written by a wide gamut of professionals. I personally have researched a never-ending list of books by gurus on the topic, works from which I have learned a great deal. Consequently, I am grateful to God for giving me the opportunity to serve in the editorial field.

Yet, this work by Dr. Daniel Villa —Siren Songs, seven stories applied to marriage—has literally enchanted me, because of its good taste in combining basic Scriptural truths with wisdom distilled from universal literature, so little known today. The author has selected some well-known old sayings and stories from ancient universal literature, and skillfully combines them with texts from Holy Scripture, to illustrate the Christian principles that must be the foundation for an excellent marital relationship.

Dr. Villa's book is written in a simple, pleasing style, and is well documented. His main concern is to help people whose marriages that are passing through dark valleys. The development is skillful and compassionate, and keeps the reader involved because it is impregnated with sound doctrine inspired by the Bible, the manual of faith and conduct for the believer. This book will serve as a guide for believers and marriages that wish to practice an effective and holy lifestyle.

This book contains instruction essential for a good marriage, points like commitment, mutual love, mutual forgiveness, mutual respect and consideration for the spouse. You will also learn about the negative effects of vengeance, bitterness and hatred in marital relations.

Dr. Villa is a well-qualified pastor, speaker and professional counselor who has practiced his profession for 30 years. This book is the result of his daily work, in which he has seen many dysfunctional homes transformed by the Word of God and by his objective professional guidance.

Siren Songs, seven stories applied to marriage is a work that has captivated my heart by its accurate and brilliant presentation. It has enriched me greatly, and I have no hesitation in recommending it to others. It is a very insightful book and my recommendation is that you read it with your spouse, not only for your benefit, dear reader, but also for that of your spouse and family: the family of God.

Nahúm Sáez
Editor

Introduction

What will be the future of our marriage? Are we building a future together or are we heading towards a failing marriage? Are the days, months, or years that we live together, uniting or separating us? Will we become a statistic in a few years? Will we be one of the marriages that end in divorce? Will our children be added to the long list of those without a father or a mother figure at home? Is there any hope? Of course there is!

The marriage crisis is intense and is growing like an epidemic. Fifty percent (50%) of families in the United States consist of second time unions. The current average duration of a marriage is seven (7) years, and one of every two marriages ends in divorce. Seventy five percent (75%) of the people that divorce will remarry. It is estimated that approximately sixty-six percent (66%) of couples who have remarried and have children from their first marriage will separate. Fifty percent (50%) of the sixty million children under age thirteen live with only one biological parent and their new partner.

We desperately need to value our marriage and work on it every day. This book is written with the purpose of offering the public not only a useful tool, but at the same time an appealing and easy-to-read book. In it we use stories and popular expressions that are a part of our everyday vocabulary.
Jesus used short stories to illustrate great and profound truths. The parables were based on things well known by his listeners. They were easy to remember, as the

---

[1] Nos divorciamos.com. Las alarmantes estadísticas del divorcio. http://www.nosdivorciamos.com/?quien=bW9kdWxvPWludGVybmEmdGFibGE9YXJ0aWN1bG8mb3BjaW9uPTE3 BjaW9uPTE3 (1/16/14) (January 16, 2014).

13

teachings were communicated in an entertaining, and almost indirect way. These biblical truths remained embedded in the minds of the listeners as the stories were recalled.

In using these stories, we are not necessarily endorsing the stories themselves. We are simply taking advantage of the fact that they are generally well known. They are being used as a resource for improving our married life.

Your family is your best and biggest investment, and therefore your marriage must be its central point. Here you will find fresh resources with a strong biblical foundation that will help you in strengthening your marriage. Each story discusses a topic that is relevant today, with practical applications. They are told in a charming style for easy reading, alone or as a couple.

Chapter 1

Milk, bacon and eggs
Total Commitment

*"Husbands, love your wives,
just as Christ loved the church
and gave himself up for her"
Ephesians 5:25 (NIV).*

Milk, bacon and eggs
Total Commitment

One of those stories that has been handed down by our grandparents states that there were various animals on a farm who were discussing whether to celebrate their owner's birthday. They were excited, talking about all the ways that they could praise their lord and master. The hen, joyfully clucking, said she would bring one dozen fresh eggs. After praising her lord and master for a while and saying how kind he was, the cow said she could offer all the milk needed for the celebration. The pig knew how much his lord and master loved having milk, bacon and eggs for breakfast, and exclaimed with a gesture of discontentment: "Well don't count on me, I don't like parties!"

In order to obtain the ingredients for a milk, bacon and eggs breakfast, we need the participation of the cow, the hen and the pig. The three animals all agreed in acquiring the ingredients needed for the breakfast. Note that without the presence and collaboration of these three animals the breakfast could never be prepared.

However, when we consider the level of commitment of each participant for the final product, we see that the participation of each is not equal. Although the celebration would require the presence, effort, discomfort and perhaps pain of the cow and the hen –if they desired–, their level of commitment was not as high as that required of the pig.

17

For the cow and the hen doing their part was relatively easy, because it did not require total commitment. Their participation was nothing new or out of the ordinary. It was basically what they did everyday, provide for breakfast. Therefore, in offering their contributions for this special occasion, they would not really be making an extreme or unusual effort.

When looking at the pig's story, we can immediately see that his situation is different. Only the pig is totally committed to the breakfast for his owner. The pig is the only one who would be making a true sacrifice in this occasion. To be precise, the illustration on the previous page does not really do any justice for the pig. He would not only be losing a leg when participating in the breakfast but would also die. He is the only one whose commitment to the breakfast plan is total or absolute.

I once heard the renowned speaker and writer, Camilo Cruz talk about complete commitment using the illustrations of eggs and bacon. He said: "For the pig, bacon and eggs is the philosophy of life. The pig sacrifices his life for the bacon and eggs."

Likewise, we should give or do our best in any endeavor that we embark, or in every cause that we embrace. The success or failure of what we do is in part determined by the commitment and disposition to pursue our objectives or goals. Why do many students abandon school? Why do some students never finish college? Why are we discouraged by a business? Why don't we finish writing that book? Why don't we reach  our dreams? Why do marriages fail? The response is the same in all of these cases. Beyond the difficulties

THE COMMITMENT THAT WE HAVE TO OUR TASK WILL MAKE THE DIFFERENCE.

that these tasks implicate, beyond the obstacles and demands that we are faced with, our level of commitment is the only thing that will make the difference.

Let us define commitment. The definition of this term states as follows:

> "The word commitment is derived from the Latin word comprimissum and is used to describe an obligation that you have contracted or a given word... It is said that a person is committed to something when they fulfill their obligations with what has been proposed or has been entrusted. This means they live, plan and act wisely in order to complete projects, have a family, do well at work, complete their studies, etc. A person is considered truly committed to a project when the actions are directed towards reaching the objective beyond what is expected".[2]

In carefully examining the expression "total commitment", it is worth asking whether it is redundant, that is to say an unnecessary repetition of words. Commitment is not really a commitment unless it is complete. Considering the issues we have with commitment, let us continue using the phrase "total commitment".

One of the biggest enemies that our society must face today is the loss or lack of commitment. As a consequence we see a great number of lives living without a purpose and without clear goals. This problem is so abundant that apparently it has turned into a philosophy of life. We have students, families, relationships, citizens, and believers (Christians) who do not have a sense commitment.

---

[2] Definicion.de. compromiso: http://definicion.de/compromiso/. (October 18, 2013).

19

In his book *Character, freedom and commitment,* *(Carácter, libertad y compromiso),* Alfonso Aguiló affirms: "To avoid commitment is to evade reality. Commitment is inevitable, life is full of commitments: with the family, with our profession, social, personal, legal and many other instances. Life is opting and acquiring links.He who attempts to opt out and not commit is not free. Heisaprisonerofhisindecisions".[3]

Commitment requires an under standing of what we are accepting. It is necessary to know the extent of our commitments, the requirements, and obligations that they entail beforehand. Without such understandings, there can be no obligations, or real and sincere commitments to a cause. We need to know what we are committing to and what is expected of us.

We must fight against the desires to be weak and relaxed, the economical limitations, regulations and the bureaucracy of the process. The list is endless. Physical limitations, mental difficulties that we impose upon life's limitations and ourselves must be evaluated. We should not overlook the selfishness, evil and the will of all those involved in the situation. We must remember that all these things, from the smallest to the largest, are all present in the process of life. Yet there are those that succeed under these circumstances. There are those that manage to make a difference. What makes the difference? The difference depends on the level of commitment that we have made for the cause and our commitment with one another.

[3] Alfonso Aguiló. Carácter, libertad, compromiso. http://www.interrogantes. net/Caracter-libertad-compromiso/ menu-id-22.html. (January 3, 2014).

There is not one single thing that I can think of that one cannot accomplish if you are willing to commit to it one hundred percent. Do not make a list of unrealistic goals, dreams and ideas to which we are not truly committed. There are many stories of accomplishments and triumphs that initially seemed impossible but were made possible. Every single person involved in these situations has carved the words "total commitment" in blood and fire in their lives... John Maxwell said: *"People don't really know whether they are committed to something until they face adversity."* [4]

What is your role, in regards to your marriage? Using the illustration above, which of the commitments of the cow, hen or pig represents yours? Apparently the cow is the least committed. The hen makes a bigger effort, but the pig is totally committed. Again, what is your role in your marriage? Think about it for a moment.

It is clear that we are not committed on many occasions. We will express it without hesitation. In other situations we believe we are committed but that is not the case. What are you committed to? Let us see if we can find out.

EVERYBODY GETS MARRIED HOPING THAT IT WILL LAST FOREVER, BUT THEY HAVE NOT DECIDED TO MAKE IT WORK.

Someone once said that everybody gets married hoping that it will last forever, but they have not decided to make it work. The difference lies between the desire and a firm decision, or the total commitment to maintain the relationship. Obviously, both must have the same level of commitment. What is your situation? Are you like the hen or the cow?

---

[4] John Maxwell. The 17 Essential Qualities of a Team Player (Nashville: Thomas Nelson Publishers, 2002) 45

We need to play the role of the pig. Congratulations if you are already doing this. Marriage must be faced with total, absolute commitment. We must give our lives for it, in order to fully enjoy living in it. I'm referring to treating your spouse like royalty, so that you can receive the same special treatment. It means giving up everything else, in order to give that person the first place in our human relationship. This is total commitment.

Marriage should be compared to the Olympic athlete who intentionally refuses entertainments, pleasures, work, or anything else that would consume his time, and solely dedicates himself to the meticulous practice of his sport. He knows that this is the only way that he can be ready to make the maximum effort. His commitment to himself, to his team, and to his country causes him to intentionally put aside everything else in order to achieve his Olympic dream.

If this is followed for a sport, and not criticized, why should we consider it an extraordinary effort when we do the same to preserve the most intimate and important relationship of life in a healthy condition? The truth is that we don't really appreciate marriage or give it the value it requires.

We need to start a marriage with the determination that it will last a lifetime. We should know that in order for a long-term commitment to become successful, we should look at it from a present point of view. Today I will be faithful. Today I will make my greatest, and best effort. I will show love today. Today I will be understanding. I will forgive today. Today my love will cover a multitude of sins. Today I will go the extra mile. Today I will not be resentful. I will be kind and affectionate today. Today I will tell my spouse how much I love him or her. Today, today...

I remember that in my town, the small grocery stores would have a sign that said, "No credit offered today. Yes, credit will be offered tomorrow." Every day the sign said the same thing, because it placed the emphasis on the present day. Today I will give my marriage the utmost. Today I will think of how I can please my family. Today I will renew my commitment to put my family first. Today I will take time to listen to the members of my family. Today...

The ministry *FamilyLife* and its Spanish-language version, *Impacto Familiar*, hold events called *"A weekend to remember."* One of the topics covered is *Five threats to the unity of marriage.* One of these threats states: *"Couples entering marriage equipped only with the world's pattern will find their oneness threatened."*[5] The model that the society offers, consists of an equal parts commitment.

The young couple accepts this model without any prior thoughts or preconceived notions. The understanding is that each member will enter the marriage contributing fifty per cent. Thus together they will have one hundred per cent of the investment that the business we call "marriage" requires. Sadly, it does not work that way, and the alarming divorce statistics prove this.

The business called marriage, contrary to any other commercial business, demands that the partners each contribute one hundred per cent, not just fifty per cent. When I contribute only fifty per cent, consciously or unconsciously I commit myself to only fifty per cent. That is, that I am responsible for only fifty per cent of the success of the marriage. I am responsible for only

---

[5] FamilyLife. Weekend to remember: conference manual (Little Rock: Christian Life Incorporated, 2003), p. 32.

fifty per cent of the faithfulness to the marriage. I am responsible for only fifty per cent of the affection shown in the relationship. I am responsible for only fifty per cent of the attention and care that we lavish on one another. If the marriage should fail, then I would be at fault, at most, for only fifty per cent of the blame.

This fifty per cent may sound reasonable to some people - equal shares - because it emphasizes that marriage involves two people, each of whom commits to do his or her share. Take my word, when I tell you that marriage does not work this way. Think about a business that hires someone for a half-time position. What is the definition of a half time position in this business? Is it the time that the employee gives to the business, or his commitment to it? Wouldn't you expect your half-time employee to devote one hundred per cent of his ability and dedication to it? Would you, on the other hand, be satisfied with only fifty per cent?

In the same manner, would you not expect this employee to give one hundred per cent of his honesty, one hundred per cent of his efforts during his time at work, one hundred per cent of his abilities and knowledge, as well as one hundred per cent of his attention? Wouldn't you expect the same commitment from a full-time employee? Yes, we would expect the same level of commitment to the business. If we expect such commitment from an employee, why would we expect marriage to work if we give it only fifty percent?

Think about this... is your marriage a half-time or a full-time commitment? Your answer, please. You're right! It is full-time. It's one hundred per cent. Why do we think it can work if we commit to only fifty per cent? Doesn't marriage demand total loyalty? Can I attain this if I commit to only fifty per cent fidelity? Total fidelity demands total commitment. There is no other way. Marriage requires a one hundred per cent commitment. Maxwell also says, "If you want a solid team, it being a business, social club, marriage or a voluntary organization, you should have players who are firmly committed to the team."[6]

The fifty per cent arrangement is a clear manifestation of human selfishness. This attitude loudly declares that, "if you don't do your part, I won't do mine." "If you don't talk to me, I won't talk to you." If you don't forgive me, I won't forgive you." "If you won't... I won't either." So the relationship is deadlocked, because neither of the two will go beyond the fifty per cent line. Neither one will swallow their pride or make sacrifices for their own good and their relationship.

Another problem with this arrangement is that we never know whether the other person is really doing his fifty per cent. If we were to ask the husband, he might say that he is giving eighty per cent and that his wife is only giving twenty percent. In all likelihood, if we were to ask her, the wife's answer would be as egotistical and unrealistic as his.

If you are married, and have not fully committed yourself to this relationship at this point, change right now. Analyze every aspect of your marriage. See which aspects are working and which are not. Stop looking for excuses, stop blaming the other person. Don't try to get your spouse to change; make the changes yourself. Notice those areas in which you were only giving a part of yourself and change your attitude. Look at the other areas in which you were really giving fifty per cent, which was the limit,

---

[6] Maxwell, op. cit. p. 34.

25

and start contributing the maximum to your relationship. Don't expect someone else to come and do it, it's up to you. So do it, do it today. You don't need to give a lot of explanations. Just start making the changes. Begin to be the person that you can be in your marriage. Forget that self-imposed selfishness and stubbornness which has become your response to the attitudes that your partner has acquired. Just begin to give your all. Nothing less than that, just your all. Have nothing to do with the role of the cow or the hen. You must play the role of the pig. All or nothing!

Far from being a breakfast of milk with bacon and eggs, a marriage should be presented as a stew with three different kinds of meat. The stew should be cooked with beef, pork, and chicken. That is to say, a dish in which all the donors contributed everything they had to give. One in which each participant gave his one hundred per cent. Marriage is like that, it demands your life, in its entirety. It is a total and unreserved commitment to the person we love and with whom we want to spend the rest of our life.

Total commitment, or playing the role of the pig, can only be compared to love. The person who truly loves commits himself totally to the loved one and to the relationship between the two. Yes, to love is to truly commit yourself. To love is to give yourself completely to your partner.

Let's see what the Scripture says. In Ephesians 5:25 we read, *"Husbands, love your wives, just as Christ loved the church and gave himself up for her."* For me, this is the greatest request that can be asked of a married man: to come to love his wife as Jesus Christ loved the Church. Let us ask ourselves: How did Christ love the Church? The same verse tells us that, *"He gave his life for her."* So we see that Jesus loved the Church with unconditional love that included sacrifice. It is a love that is unselfish, loyal, and committed, that puts our spouse in first place.

Jesus told His disciples, *"A new command I give you: Love one another. As I have loved you, so you must love one another."*[7] This command goes beyond the one that tells us to love our neighbor as ourselves. If Jesus had loved us as he loved himself, he would not have died for us. He loved us more than he loved himself, since he gave his life for us.

Jesus left us a new commandment. He asked us to love the same way that he loved. This is the highest form of love that is possible to have. It means to give yourself for the other person. It means to give yourself completely, even to the extent of giving up your life, as he did. Is this not total, complete commitment?

Most of the problems and inconveniences in marriages arise because we will not allow our rights to be violated, either by real or imaginary actions. When we assume the biblical attitude of loving our spouse as Jesus loved the Church, just by attempting it, we see that it covers a multitude of faults. If we assume this attitude, we will be much more willing to understand and to show empathy. This example is telling us to walk in another person's shoes and to try to see things as the other person sees them. We should attempt to do this before we defend ourselves, even when we are not really being attacked.

---

[7] John 14:34, NIV

José José sings a song called "Amar y querer" (To love and to want) in which the author, Manuel Alejandro, correctly points out the commitments that love has us do. The song says:

Almost all of us know how to want,
But few of us know how to love.
Loving and wanting are not the same thing;
To love is to suffer, to want is to enjoy.

He who loves commits to follow,
He who loves gives his life.
He who wants commits to live, and
Never to suffer, and never suffer.

He who loves cannot reason,
Everything he gives, everything he gives,
He who wants tries to forget, and
Never to cry, and never cry.

 Wanting may soon be over,
Love knows no end.
We all know how to want,
But very few know how to love.

Love is the heavens and light,
Love is fulfillment complete,
As the ocean without any end,
Loving is glory and peace.
Loving is glory and peace.

Wanting is the flesh and the flower;
It is seeking the dark hidden place;
It is to bite, to scratch, and to kiss.
Wanting is fleeting desire;
Wanting is fleeting desire.

28

Wanting may soon be over,
Love knows no end.
We all know how to want,
But very few know how to love.[8]

Jesus is our greatest living example. He sacrificed his life by dying on the cross for us because of the great love he felt for us. Jesus was totally committed to his plan of salvation. He wanted to provide a way by which we could be forgiven and freed from the sin that bonded us to eternal condemnation. Jesus was born with this purpose. He became a man in order to take our place and pay our debt. A debt that could never have been paid through our own efforts.
Jesus faced temptations on the way to the cross. He remained firm and faithful to His cause, in spite of the mocking and misunderstandings of His own family. He went to the cross, knowing that this was the only way he could save us. His eternal love caused Him to commit himself totally and completely. Let us do the same, just as He did. Everything changes when we give one hundred per cent. So, let's do it today!

We will conclude this chapter by referring to an old saying used in the Dominican culture. This saying is used to point out that a person wants something but has little or no commitment. It goes like this: "You like to pick the low-hanging mangos." That is, the person says he is committed and willing to do his part, but wants to make the least possible effort. The saying comes from a "décima" (a ten-line stanza) by Juan Antonio Alix entitled, "The low-hanging mangos." Two of the verses say:
Don Juan Martín Garata,
a person of high rank,

---

[8] Oswaldo Paez. Amar y querer. http://elblogdelbolero.wordpress.com/2008/06/25/manuel-alejandro-el-compositor-del-amor/(October 12, 2013).

likes mangos very much,
because they are a desirable fruit.
But to scramble up the tree,
and out onto the small branches,
running all kinds of risks—
since that is so dangerous,
he finds it more delicious
to pick the low-hanging mangos.

Don Martín also says
that he likes chestnuts,
but only if someone else
takes them from the pan
and peels them properly.
But to burn his fingers,
putting them in the flame,
that is not what is called
picking the low-hanging mangos.[9]

As we can see, Don Martín Garata liked to enjoy everything without committing himself at all. In marriage there is no room for the attitude of "picking the low-hanging mangos." It is all or nothing!

Questions for discussion:
1. Under what conditions would you consider divorce an option?
   a) Incompatibility.
   b) Incurable mental illness.
   c) Infidelity.
   d) Financial problems.
   e) Any of the above.
   f) None of the above.

[9] Juan Antonio Alix, Décimas dominicanas de ayer y de hoy (Santo Domingo: Publicaciones América, 1986), p. 36.

2. With which of the following statements do you identify most closely?
   a) My place is with my spouse.
   b) My place is with my children.
   c) I should live my own life.
   d) Any of the above.
   e) None of the above.

3. When you return home after a one-week trip and your family, including your mother, is waiting for you, whom do you kiss first?
   a) My spouse.
   b) My mother.
   c) My children.
   d) The dog.
   e) None of the above.

4. If you felt you have stopped loving your spouse what would you do?
   a) Get a divorce. I could not live with someone I do not love.
   b) I would find a way to revive the love because marriage is forever.
   c) I would give myself a chance to start over and if it does not work out, get a divorce; but not without giving ourselves another chance.
   d) None of the above.
   e) I don't know what I would do.

5. A survey showed that one of every two people surveyed would be unfaithful if their spouse would never find out. What is your opinion about this?

6. Please select one of the following statements:
   a) Marriage is a sacred institution and is
      for life.
   b) Marriage should be for a lifetime but
      sometimes this is not possible.
   d) Marriage is for a lifetime if you have the right
      spouse.
   e) Marriage will last as long as there is
      love.
   f) Marriage is a trap. I don't know how I
      fell for it.

7. Definitions of marriage. Select the one that matches
   yours.
   a) It is the only war in which you sleep with the
      enemy.
   b) It serves to solve problems you would
      have never had if you had remained single.
   c) Mathematically: it adds affection,
      subtracts liberties, multiplies responsibilities,
      and divides possessions.
   e) None of the above.

8. If your spouse and your mother are drowning and you
   can save only one person, whom would you pick?
   a) Obviously, my mother.
   b) Obviously, my spouse.
   c) Neither of them.
   d) I would not know what to do.

Chapter 2

The Trojan Horse
Protect your marriage

"And no wonder, for Satan himself masquerades as an angel of light"
2 Corinthian 11:14 (NIV).

The Trojan Horse
Protect your marriage

The Greeks and Trojans were fighting a bloody war that had been going on for nine years. The Greeks had already lost their great defender Achilles, who had appeared to be immortal. He was eventually wounded in one of his heels and died. This war, as senseless as all other wars, had begun over the love of a woman. Helen of Sparta, the wife of the king, had run away with Paris, a prince of Troy. People today still wonder whether a city called Troy ever existed. They question whether this war was real, or whether it was only a figment of the imagination of Homer, who tells about these conflicts in his epic poems "The Iliad" and "The Odyssey."

With the death of Achilles and after ten years of war, the Greeks were discouraged and ready to withdraw. In spite of their enormous army and their even greater tenacity, they had not been able to conquer Troy. The city and its inhabitants remained safe and defiant behind their strong, indestructible walls. No effort or military strategy had been effective. The Greeks had lost all hope. They consulted their magician Calchas. Calchas told them that they could not win the war unless they brought Neoptolemus, the son of Achilles to fight for them. Nothing happened. By order of the same seer, they also brought the bones of one of their leaders and an image of one of their gods. Even so, the Greeks were not able to breach the walls of Troy.

One day the magician Calchas watched as a falcon pursued a dove. Trying to escape, the dove hid in the crack of a rock. The falcon continued to fly over the area. The dove would not come out. The falcon then pretended to go away, and hid from the dove's sight. After waiting a long time without seeing her attacker, the dove emerged from her hiding place, and was caught by the falcon. After telling his companions about what he had seen, Calchas concluded that they should not continue to attack the walls of Troy by force. They would have to think or come up with some stratagem to take the city over. After this, Odysseus conceived the plan of building a large horse. He hides the best warriors inside of the horse. Other versions of the story say the plan was elaborated by Athena.

With instructions from Odysseus, Epeios built an enormous wooden horse. It was hollow inside, in order to hold and hide the soldiers. Once the wooden figure was built, Odysseus and 39 other Greek warriors crept into the horse. The remainder of the Greek fleet withdrew, leaving the horse behind. Sinon, was the only man who stayed behind.

When the Trojans saw that the Greeks had left, they came out from their city to see the immense wooden horse. Sinon led them to believe that the wooden horse was a talisman being used to win the war. He also told them that his fellow soldiers had abandoned him, and that the Trojans could now use the same talisman for their own benefit. So the Trojans believed Sinon's lies and took possession of the horse to offer it to their gods. They did not realize that it was a trick of the Greeks to get inside their city. Sinon accompanied them.

The horse was of immense size. It was built that way so that the Trojans would not be able to get it into the city. They had to tear down part of the city wall in order to take it inside. They believed that if they stole the Greek's "talisman", they would obtain a definitive victory in the war. Cassandra, who had the gift of prophecy, was opposed to bringing the horse into the city. She knew that this would mean the end of Troy, but no one listened to her. That very night the Trojans celebrated what they thought was their victory by bringing the horse into the city, with all the effort necessary to accomplish this. When Troy fell asleep under the influence of alcohol, Sinon released the Greek warriors from the horse. They opened the city gates and the invading force entered and massacred the Trojans.[10]

We will use this story as an illustration to talk about some of the dangers that surround marriage, and some of the means that we have available to protect it.

We note that the Trojans were safe behind their city walls. No effort to harm them had been successful in ten long years. The people remained firm and united, so that their enemy was unable to destroy them. It was not until the Greeks were able to get inside the city that they achieved their objective. And the worse thing was that the Trojans themselves provided the access to the enemy. As long as they stayed inside their city they were safe.

In applying this story to marriage, we will consider two important points about marriage. First, we will speak about the walls of Troy, to refer to the walls that protect marriage and the family. Second, we will consider some "Trojan horses" that may attack our marriages today. We call this point The deception of the Greeks. We will begin with the first point.

The walls of Troy

In spite of the numerical superiority of the Greeks, and the fact that they had among them an almost immortal warrior such as Achilles -even so, in a

---

[10] Miguel García Álvarez, The Trojan Horse, http://recuerdos depandora.com/mitos/el-caballo-de troya (June 27, 2013).

war that lasted ten years they had not been able to conquer the city of Troy. According to some historians, the walls of Troy were not so imposing as those of other cities of the era, but they were built with the advances of Hittite engineering. The walls were between seven and eight meters high and four-and-one-half meters thick.[11]

This makes me think that it was the ideal combination of well-built walls and the unity of the people that enabled them to withstand ten years of siege. Let me ask you: What makes a marriage secure? What is the strength of a marriage? What qualities can sustain it? Please think about your own marriage. What are its foundations and its strong points? What gives it cohesion and firmness? Upon what or upon whom does your relationship rest?

In the same way that the city of Troy was safe and protected by its walls, so our relationship should be protected by strong walls, to resist the attack of enemies and detractors of our marriage. They intend to destroy, or at the least damage, our relationship, and they will succeed if we let them. Walls are built for two purposes: to mark the limits of a property and to protect it. From our point of view, the walls that protect marriage are built upon three basic elements: The covenants made by the couple; the commandments of mutuality; and Biblical principles.

Covenants, agreements, and promises

These form the foundation upon which the relationship is built. The couple meets and begins their relationship when they become engaged. The path from engagement to the marriage altar will be paved with promises,

---

[11] José I. Lago. How was Troy? (¿Cómo era Troya?) http://www.historialago.com/leg_troy_01015_comoera_01.htm (June 28, 2013).

agreements, and covenants that will define the distinctive characteristics of this couple and their relationship. In fact, without these agreements and covenants, whether implicit or written, the relationship will die. These promises, agreements, and dreams, confirmed by the passage of time, give life to the marriage.

Likewise, with the passage of years and facing the challenges of life, it is these old but updated covenants which will enable the couple to remain strong against the storms of life. If one of the two breaks or forgets the covenants, agreements, and promises that established the relationship, it will be at the mercy of the enemies which seek to destroy it. Just as the city of Troy was built within an area enclosed by its enormous walls, which delimited the territory that belonged to the Trojans, and which they were prepared to defend with their lives, in marriage these covenants are the walls which protect it. The married couple has a territory to defend—their home.

Therefore, let us be faithful to the promises, covenants, and agreements we have made. Keep them fresh and up to date. As we already have said, every long-term promise must be reduced to the twenty-four hours of the present day. For example, "I will be faithful to you all my life," must be translated as, "Today I will be faithful to my spouse."

When the writer of the Biblical Book of Proverbs counsels his son against the wiles of the adulterous woman, he says in 5:18, "May you rejoice in the wife of your youth." This saying, which is almost a prayer, refers to faithfulness to those first promises, to the covenants and agreements we made long ago in the springtime of our relationship. Our God is a God of covenants. Israel, God's people, had problems when they violated or forgot their covenants with God. Many times God showed mercy, forgiving His unfaithful people, because of His regard for His covenants. This should encourage us to be faithful to our promises and fulfill them. If we disregard the promises we have made, it will be like allowing a huge hole to penetrate the walls which protect our marriage.

Commands of mutuality

When we speak of commands of mutuality, we are referring to the various attitudes which each member of a couple or family should have, and which the Bible teaches are requirements for proper relationships. The list is long, but for our purposes we will concentrate on the three that we believe are essential, and which will sustain the life of the couple that practices them daily.

1. Mutual love
Peaceful and loving coexistence never happens by chance. If we want to live this way, we will have to work for it. Living together, in close contact, tends to produce friction between people. These points of friction must be faced wisely. The goal is not to avoid all conflict; rather it is to face it constructively.

Do you know why we add oil to automobile engines? Yes, I know that if we don't do this, the motor will burn up. But why will it burn up? Yes, I know that it will overheat, but why? Before I drive you crazy, I will tell you where I'm heading. The engine will overheat because of friction. We must understand that when we speak of friction, it doesn't mean that the parts are striking against one another. Rather, we mean that the parts are moving very rapidly, in very close proximity to one another.
The oil reduces this "friction" and maintains the temperatures at safe levels. The better the lubricant, the

better results we will obtain. If you know something about automobiles, you will know that these lubricants come with various additives that promise to protect and extend the life of your engine, without reducing the revolutions that it has to produce. I hope I haven't bored you with this, but it is important to illustrate and understand the concept.

You will have noticed that it is easier to get along well with people who are far away from us. This is so because there is less friction, less contact, less communication between us. Families, and couples in particular, are called to live together. This means that they must reveal themselves as they really are, and live their lives in the same environment.

We want every family and every couple to grow and reach its potential. This is like saying that they will reach a high velocity in a short distance. If this is true, and it is, we should not be surprised when friction happens, or that the temperature occasionally rises in the relationship or the family. We need a lubricant that will enable us to maintain a reasonable temperature without sacrificing the development of each member of the relationship.

Remember, the better the additives in the lubricant, the better the protection we will have. I believe that the essential additives in relationships are: love, respect, and forgiveness. These will enable you to maintain your relationship at the highest level, because they will help you to deal with the high temperatures that two human beings living together may generate. Two people who may be compared to two powerful lamps which must unite their beams and together produce the most brilliant and beautiful beam of light, which one of them alone could not produce. Two worlds that are called to live as

41

one; two hearts that must beat as one.

The love of which we speak is much greater and more precious than the common sentiment that is sold to us with shop-worn, unrealistic phrases, the kind of sentiment that we show only when we are feeling well and satisfied. That sentiment is conditional and heavy with selfishness, a sentiment that runs and hides when faced with any hint of difficulty.

In contrast, we need to know that love is a decision. Love means a commitment of the will. Love is sacrifice. Listen to how the Bible describes it:

> *Love is patient, love is kind. It does not envy, it does not boast, it is not proud. It is not rude, it is not self-seeking, it is not easily angered, it keeps no record of wrongs. Love does not delight in evil but rejoices with the truth. It always protects, always trusts, always hopes, always perseveres. Love never fails....And now these three remain: faith, hope and love. But the greatest of these is love.* [12]

As you read these lines, dear reader, I invite you to evaluate yourself by answering these questions: Do I really love? Am I accustomed to be impatient and seldom longsuffering and kind to my wife? Am I envious, presumptuous, arrogant or crude? Am I frequently irritated and irritable? Do I always try to win? Is it hard for me to forgive? Please reflect on these things. I mean that you should stop reading and meditate on your relationship. The purpose of this list is not to prove that you do not love your mate; on the contrary, these are important points in which we should grow as persons and as a couple.

If you answered "yes" to one or more of the previous questions, what will you do about it? We have already

---

[12] 1 Corinthians 13:4-7, NIV.

said that love demands that we do something on behalf of our relationship and of the loved one. Let me suggest the following exercise: In prayer ask God to bring to your mind the challenges to growth that you face (the places where you are failing), and make a list of them. Make a plan of action. How can I act differently at this point? Your plan of action should have two parts: points A and B. Part A will be to face your spouse and confess your carelessness, sin, and lack of interest in the points that you have listed. You must ask forgiveness for each one of them.

Part B will consist of thinking about how you will work on these weak points. For example, "If one of my problems is that I am too vulgar, I will try to speak with respect, love, and refinement." Get up and do it without delay. It does us no good to have a plan if we don't put it into action. Remember that there are forces that work against the success of your marriage, which will resist you so that you do not fulfill your plan. Pray for strength and willpower. And execute your plan!

It seems that love, like faith, is a verb. That means that it generates action and demands action. There is no congruence between loving and remaining indifferent to the problems and demands of the relationship. Love moves me to do or say something in support of that relationship and the person I love. Likewise, it appears that the ways in which we usually treat one another and the demands of true love are simply incompatible.

Love must be expressed. We can do this with words and actions. In general, women need to hear that they are loved and are special to their husbands. We men should not be stingy in expressing all kinds of verbal appreciation for our wives. Other women prefer to see

43

some type of action, to prove and support those words. Perhaps it may be something as simple as helping with the domestic chores, or caring for the children, or doing something else that is useful. Flowers and special gifts on the usual occasions will also let them know that they are important to us. The love of the husband stimulates the respect of the wife.

2. Mutual respect.
The apostle Paul, after telling the husband that he should love his wife, speaks to the wife. I can imagine that the women were expecting to hear the same command or suggestion. But it is interesting to note that he leaves them with their mouths open when he says, *"And you wives, respect your husbands."* What? They would say; then we don't have to love them? Just a moment, Paul would answer, that's not correct. Of course you should love your husband. The way it works is that the wife expresses her love for her husband by means of the respect she has for him. As Dr. Emerson Eggerichs stated: *"Without love, she reacts without respect. Without respect, he reacts without love."*[13] And the opposite is also true: *"His love evokes respect in her. Her respect evokes love in him."*[14]

Let's talk for a moment about respect. In the light of Biblical teaching the characteristics of love include respect and forgiveness. If we act disrespectfully, it will be hard for us to convince others that we truly love. Impatience, rudeness, and coarseness grow and develop in the absence of respect, and of course, of love. If we act harshly and irritably it will be very difficult for us to respect the other person. Lack of consideration leads to lack of respect. Harsh, hurtful words, gestures of contempt, and carelessness about the relationship

[13] Emerson Eggerichs, Love & respect, (Nashville: Thomas Nelson, 2000), p. 36.
[14] Ibid., 17.

constitute lack of respect.

Respect is essential for men. Those who understand human nature point to respect as one of the basic emotional needs of men. A man cannot understand love without respect, when it is directed toward himself. The man who does not sense that he is respected at home will prefer to spend more time at work, if he is respected there. If the woman shows disrespect to her husband in public, he will feel profoundly shamed and deeply wounded. Any fault or weakness expressed in public will hit him like a dagger thrust.

If you say, "This man is a good-for-nothing," he will feel as thought he were falling into an endless abyss. He will feel humiliated—that his life has no purpose. He will think that nothing is worth his effort, and that he is wasting time in this relationship.

On the other hand, if he hears you say, "My husband is a good provider," or "He is a great father," or "I am proud of my husband," this will make him feel like Superman. It will give him new strength, which he will eagerly use to care for the relationship. The Bible commands the man to be strong and to treat his beloved as "the weaker partner." It says just that in 1 Peter 3:7: "Husbands, in the same way be considerate as you live with your wives, and treat them with respect as the weak er partner and as heirs with you of the gracious gift of life, so that nothing will hinder your prayers."

An abused woman feels despised and used. In respecting his wife, the husband respects himself. A wife who feels loved and respected will act with love and respect for her husband.

3. Mutual forgiveness.

Forgiveness provides the oxygen that the relationship needs for healthy living. Lack of appreciation, misunderstandings, half truths, things not understood by our partner that we consider obvious, things like these can poison the relationship. The atmosphere of the home becomes charged with this toxic cloud that is poisoning us day by day. The more we are exposed to it, the greater the harm we suffer. Forgiveness has the power to clear the air and permit the sun of understanding to shine upon the couple.

A typical example of this environmental contamination are the partial circles in our communication. The couple had a disagreement for some reason that usually is something small and easily dealt with. But instead of facing the problem and resolving it, we try to forget it and act as though nothing had happened. These are partial, unclosed circles, because we don't take the time or trouble to close them. Each of these cases is stored in the mind and heart of the couple, or one partner, forming that toxic cloud that poisons us.

When one visits a home that is in this condition, one can sense that the atmosphere is tense. Although things may appear normal, the simple daily activities of the home appear to be very hard to accomplish. Communication is reduced to a minimum; smiles disappear, looks that wound replace those that caress. Once again, greater exposure produces greater contamination. Simply change the atmosphere. Yes, open the window of forgiveness and allow it to refresh the entire atmosphere of the home. Close the open circle by confronting your spouse in love, and make peace.

My favorite saying for married couples is "Don't let the sun go down upon your wrath." I remember once, when

I was working for the Bible Society in the Dominican Republic, I was asked to write a note on a card we were preparing for a recently married couple, both of them employees. I wrote for them, "Let not the sun go down upon your wrath." I remember this very clearly, because I failed to explain that this was my desire for them in their relationship.

Some time later the couple came to me, somewhat ashamed, asking whether I was upset with them, and whether I was admonishing them by means of the Bible verse that I had written. I told them warmly, No, by no means, because they were very easy to get along with, very friendly and prudent. I explained that this was the desire of my heart for them regarding their daily life. The Bible puts it this way: *In your anger do not sin: Do not let the sun go down while you are still angry, and do not give the devil a foothold.*[15]

In the light of these verses we understand that: 1) Anger is not in itself a sin. 2) We may be closer to sinning when we are angry. Or if we are angry, we should be more careful in order not to sin. 3) The debts or faults in the relationship  should be paid or resolved daily. 4) If we remain angry beyond that limit, we are giving Satan openings to attack us.

Then let us remember that forgiveness is not earned nor deserved. If someone deserves to be forgiven, we are not really dealing with forgiveness. Forgiveness is extended to the guilty.

---

[15] Ephesians 4:26-27.

And precisely for that reason, because he is guilty, we choose to forgive him. To forgive is a decision we make in obedience to the Father, in imitation of the Son, and through the power of the Holy Spirit. We want to stress that it is a decision. That is to say, I know that I should forgive; therefore I extend forgiveness.

So do not allow yourself to be governed by your feelings, but rather by the Word of God. When you grant forgiveness, your feelings will follow the decision of your will, which is to forgive.

The Biblical principles
(The couple and the Bible)

The third factor in the protective wall around the couple is the attention which they give to the Word of God. Throughout Biblical history we see God calling men and instructing them to keep His Word close. The closer they walked in God's commandments, the better their path would be. This continues to be a most important truth for every believer. If these believers decide to get married, it will be even more important for their lives that they hear the wise and holy words of God.

Psalm 19:7 -14 teaches us:
> The law of the Lord is perfect, reviving the soul. The statutes of the Lord are trustworthy, making wise the simple. The precepts of the Lord are right, giving joy to the heart. The commands of the Lord are radiant, giving light to the eyes. The fear of the Lord is pure, enduring forever. The ordinances of the Lord are sure and altogether righteous. They are more precious than gold, than much pure gold; they are sweeter than honey, than honey from the comb. By them is your servant warned;

in keeping them there is great reward. Who can discern his errors? Forgive my hidden faults. Keep your servant also from willful sins; may they not rule over me. Then will I be blameless, innocent of great transgression. May the words of my mouth and the meditation of my heart be pleasing in your sight, O Lord, my Rock and my Redeemer.

Who would attempt to acquire wisdom for life while at the same time rejecting these words? Why do we ignore divine counsel and seek human counseling? Many times during counseling couples are not asked whether they are trying to obey the instructions of the Bible. Is this not one of the first questions that a Biblical counselor should ask? How far can a couple go if they do not pay attention to the Word of God? We know that no matter what we say to them, they will not get very far.

If a couple has problems in communicating or in forgiving, do we explain to them what the Bible says about these topics? If they don't listen to God, will they be able to resolve their problem? Will they listen to us?

Dear reader, it is obligatory that we obey God and His Word if we dream of having a home that conforms to His divine will. I like to ask the people I counsel to read and practice the Biblical counsel with its practical applications that we find in Ephesians 4:22-32. If problems continue, I insist on asking whether they are practicing what they have read. The answer is always the same: No, we are not doing that. From my point of view, whenever a couple divorces or simply is not living their marriage to the fullest, the reason is that one or both of them refuses to practice the Biblical advice about living well, which in fact is not simply advice but divine commands.

If they are not willing to do this, I simply do not continue the counseling, because they are wasting their time and mine as well. If we really want to protect our marriage, it is essential that we understand, obey, and practice the divine counsel.

By joining together these three basic elements: the covenants of the couple, the commandments of mutuality, and Biblical principles, the couple builds an impenetrable wall to protect their relationship, which will make it capable of withstanding the severe and continuous attacks by their enemies. Behind this wall you can resist and obtain the victory, no matter how long the siege. But remember, do not go out beyond the security of your walls, and above all, do not bring a Trojan horse inside them.

The deception of the Greeks

The real reason this story is famous is not because of the strength of the walls of Troy, but because of the ingenious deception of the Greeks in building a colossal horse that enabled them to penetrate the city walls. What ten years of warfare had not won was achieved by cunning in a single night. This is a real revelation. Think about it: a brave, battle-hardened, well-equipped army in ten years could not conquer a city defended by a much inferior army. Neither weapons, hunger, nor witchcraft succeeded in penetrating the walls. But the deception did not have to knock down the gates, but was received with celebration and with wide-open gates. This makes me think about the power that deception has, and how effective and harmful it can be. The Trojan horse is really Greek.

Today, in the world of cybernetics, there are computer viruses called Trojan, which are disguised as advertizing or special offers, but which are really harmful viruses. Personally, this use of the term "Trojan" seems incorrect to me because the Trojans were deceived; they did not devise the deception. But it would be hard to change this usage, and if I attempt to use the term with a different meaning, it could be confusing. So I will use "Trojan" with the same meaning that you likely know, referring to a deception. Therefore, we will call Trojan any person, relationship, event, or decision that appears to be good and wholesome for the relationship or the family, but whose purpose is really to damage the couple.

According to this statement, there are men or women who are Trojan "friends." They approach one member of the couple, or even both members, and offer their "help" in a particular situation, or their "sincere friendship," but their action is really motivated by a romantic attraction to you or your spouse. Or their motive may be to harm the couple or the family in some way. We need to analyze such persons carefully, without giving in to panic or obsession; to be alert against such attacks.

As we already stated, an open frontal attack tends to unite us, but the danger of the Trojans is that they appear to be friendly and well-intentioned. They win the confidence of one or both persons in the relationship, and frequently cause division regarding the opinion that we have of them. If one member suspects or sees the possible attack, very likely the other member will discount the danger and defend the Trojan. This will cause a distraction among the sentinels of the fortress; frequently this aspect alone of the attack produces serious damage to the relationship.

How can we recognize a Trojan? Here are some suggestions. First, remember that they are Trojans. That means that they are not easy to spot. Their strength consists in remaining hidden. So pay attention to your instincts or your hunches. Don't ignore them, but do not take them for fact, either. But if you sense something, pay attention to it, or to the person who may be warning you about the danger that he foresees.

Remember that Trojans don't fight fair. They don't face us or confront us with a battle. If they did that, they would unite us. They disguise themselves to enter our camp and do us harm, because they know that from the outside they can't hurt us. So the best thing that we can do is to strengthen our intimate relationship. That way, if a Trojan does manage to get in, the damage will be minimal. If a couple loves and respects one another, if they are sincere with each other, speaking the truth and not keeping secrets, even though a Trojan may enter it will not be able to do much harm, because it operates through lies and in darkness. The more transparent the relationship, the less trouble a Trojan can cause.

Trojans are disciples of Satan, who is a master of deceit. We should not be surprised that some people allow him to use them for such purposes. The Bible says: *"And no wonder, for Satan himself masquerades as an angel of light."* [16]

---

[16] 2 Corinthians 11:14.

Questions for discussion:

1. What gives you security in your marriage? What gives it cohesiveness and strength?

2. What are the covenants, agreements, and promises? Why are they important?

3. What are the commandments of mutuality? State why they are important in your relationship with your spouse.

4. What role do Biblical principles play, and the Bible in general, in your marriage relationship?

5. Can you identify the "Trojans" that try to destroy the walls of your marriage?

Chapter 3

Burn your ships
Break harmful relationships
Reject Divorce

"For this reason a man will leave his father and mother and be united to his wife, and they will become one flesh" Genesis 2:24 (NIV)

Burn your ships
Reject Divorce

Alexander III of Macedon, better known as Alexander the Great, ruled as king from the time he was twenty years old until his death at thirty-three years of age. He conquered the Persian Empire as well as Anatolia, Phoenicia, Gaza, Syria, Egypt, Mesopotamia, Judea and many other regions.

In 335 B.C., upon arriving on the coast of Phoenicia, Alexander the Great faced one of h is greatest battles. When he disembarked, he realized that the enemy soldiers outnumbered his army three to one. His men were frightened and saw no reason to face the battle. They had lost their confidence and considered themselves defeated. Fear had overcome these invincible warriors.

After Alexander had disembarked all his men on the enemy coast, he ordered that all his ships be burned. While the ships were burning and sinking in the sea, he gathered his men and said to them: "See how the ships are burning. This is the only reason why we must win, because if we lose, we cannot return home and none of us will ever see our families again. Nor will we be able to leave this land that today we despise. We must triumph in this battle, because there is only one way home—by sea. Gentlemen, when we go home we will do so in the only possible way—in the ships of our enemies!" Alexander's army won that battle and went home on board the ships captured from the enemy.[17]

---

[17] www.ultraguia.com.ar. Burn the thips. www.ultraguia.com.ar//UltraSociales/ParaPen sar/ParaPensar09.html) (April 20, 2013).

57

Similar feats are recounted about various leaders in different battles throughout history. Take for example Agathocles, the tyrant of Syracuse (361-289 B.C.); the Emperor Julian, in his expedition against Shapur; Julius Caesar in one of his campaigns, when after crossing the Rubicon, ordered the bridge destroyed, with the famous phrase Alea jacta est (The die is cast); or William the Conqueror, when he arrived on the coast of England in 1066. [18]

But the case that is closest and best known to us is that of Hernán Cortés, in his conquest of what today is Mexico. Cortés left Cuba in 1519 with about 500 men for his expedition to Mexico. When he saw that his men were

EACH SPOUSE MUST VOLUNTARILY GIVE UP HIS OR HER INDIVIDUAL FREEDOM IN ORDER TO ENJOY ONE ANOTHER.

vacillating and indecisive and found out that some of them were planning to take a ship and return to Governor Diego Velázquez in Cuba, Cortés decided to burn his ships, destroying at the same time all hope of escape or return to Cuba. When he did this, Cortés left only one alternative to his men: to win or to die in the attempt. In this way he expressed his determination to conquer in whatever way possible, with no return.[19]

Cortés's daring decision gave to the expedition a different tone. It was no longer an exploratory journey or a tentative advance dependant on possible victory. From that moment on, they could only advance and conquer or be destroyed by the fierce, brave Indians that were defending their territory with all the weapons at their disposal. It seems that the ships were not really burned, but rather scuttled, which served the same

---

[18] El bufón digital. Burn the ships. (http://elbufondigital.blogspot.com/2008/01/quemar-las-navesquien-fu-el-primero.html. (April 20, 2013).
[19] Wikipedia. Burn the ships. http://es.wikipedia.org/wiki/Quemar_las_naves. (Abril 21, 2013).

purpose. Whatever the method, the phrase "to burn your ships" has come down to posterity. It means to win or to die. There is no turning back! Dare to make a total commitment to victory, leaving behind forever everything that could distract us or diminish our effort to our cause. In the case that concerns us, "to burn your ships" means to commit ourselves to marriage to the utmost. It means to say No to divorce.

If there is any endeavor in which we must burn our ships, it is marriage. Marriage is an exclusive relationship, for two people only. It is a fruit to be shared between two persons, an umbrella for two and no one else. Each spouse must voluntarily give up his or her individual freedom in order to enjoy one another, becoming one flesh, as the Bible expresses it. Marriage, as we have already stated, is an undertaking that requires total and complete commitment. Therefore the participants must break with any other commitment or obligation, in order to make marriage their priority.

To burn one's ships is to say that marriage has no reverse gear. And so it means a life-long commitment to strive together against every obstacle, to keep the relationship alive, fresh, and productive for both partners. The couple that has burned its ships—and both spouses need to do this—is the couple that has said No to divorce. They have the habit of not mentioning the word "divorce" in their conversations about their relationship, not even as a joke, because divorce is not an option.

When this attitude is adopted, it is understood that the couple must face challenges together, because there is no going back. But what are we talking about? What may be the possible "ships" that we must burn? How can we burn them? We will look at some of them, but you doubtless can add others.

The ship of the family

It is God Himself who tells us that marriage is the relationship that has the highest priority. It has priority over the relation with parents and with children. In Genesis 2:24 we read: *"For this reason a man will leave his father and mother and be united to his wife, and they will become one flesh."*

We notice that the text speaks of the breaking of a natural, primary relationship, one which for those reasons is very strong. We are talking about the relationship between parents and children. In the first place, this is a natural relationship.

In this relationship the children have no choice. By virtue of birth, they belong to that particular family unit. By natural process the children grow under the care of and dependent upon their parents. From them they receive love, protection, and guidance. By no choice of our own, when we become aware of our situation, as children we already have parents or guardians. This is the first relationship into which we enter.

Our parents are the first persons from whom we receive affection, and with whom we identify emotionally. We become part of a community called family. Once again, this is a natural process that tends to produce a very strong bond. Could there be another relationship of more importance than this one? The answer is Yes: the formation of a new home. Again, the Scripture says: *"For this reason a man will leave his father and mother and be united to his wife, and they will become one flesh."* That first strong relationship must yield to another, which although it will not annul the first or replace it, must take priority over it. Marriage and the relationship of the couple is the most important relationship of life. The relationship with one's spouse has *priority* over that with one's parents. It does not take the place of that first relationship, nor does it reduce the love and respect that we have for our parents. We don't go into marriage seeking another father or mother. The marriage relationship has top priority because it is with the person with whom we become "one flesh." In this new relationship a decision is central. It is not a "natural" relationship; rather it is created by a decision. We do not choose our parents or our siblings, but we usually do choose the person who will become our spouse.

It is more common than we would like to admit that many parents invite their son or daughter to return to the ship that was their home, when they learn that there is strong conflict between the spouses. *"Dear girl, don't worry; you don't have to put up with that good-for-nothing. You have a home here; here you will lack for nothing. Get a divorce; the sooner you get rid of him the better."* One would get the impression that marriage is something disposable. This is typical advice that many married people get from their parents.

As a marriage counselor, in some cases I recommend a temporary separation during which the couple continues to work on their relationship, or a quick exit when the life of one of the spouses is in danger. This is violence within the family, commonly called domestic violence. But such is usually not the case when parents make this insistent invitation. Sometimes parents refuse to accept that their

61

children are now grown up and have their own home. They do not understand that they have not lost their child; that he or she will never cease to be their child. No matter how far away they move, the relationship between father and son or daughter, and between mother and daughter or son will never be broken.

It is likely that major conflicts will arise between parents and children, or among the siblings; but they will never cease to be siblings, nor cease to be parents and children. So as someone commented, we will never hear anyone say: *There goes my ex-mother or my ex-brother*, because these relationships are unbreakable; they are blood relationships. But the case of the spouse is different. It is very common to hear: *There goes my ex-husband or ex-wife, my ex-mother-in-law, my ex-brother-in-law.* These facts show how important it is that marriage have top priority. The relationship of the couple, of marriage, is one that we must care for, cultivate, and fight to defend, because this relationship can indeed be broken.

We must abandon this "ship" with dignity and respect, always giving to our parents their position of honor. To burn this ship means to cut the umbilical cord, which may be uniting us with our parents more than is wholesome. Any intervention of the parents that upsets or damages the proper functioning of the new home is a ship which we must burn.

The ship of the children

The level of priority required by the relationship of the couple speaks loudly of its importance in the life of the persons involved in every home. We frequently hear married women say: *I will be with my children, wherever they are.* The demands of the married relationship should lead them to say: *I will be with my husband, wherever he is.* Obviously, in too many cases the reason for making this statement is the experience of a marriage relationship that is deficient, uncared for, and occasionally, abusive.

When abuse happens, we are dealing with a deformed relationship. The man takes on the role of "father," when he should be the "committed lover." Thus the roles in the relationships are confused, and the worst possible example of a father is used, the role of the "abusive father." But just as the relationship of the couple has priority over the relation with the parents, likewise it must take precedence over the relation with the children. Some parents when speaking of their children say: *They are carrying on my blood line.* But it is good to remember that the blood they carry comes from both parents; and that only with our spouse do we become one flesh.

The couple came first, then the children arrived. These children will leave, but the couple should remain together to see them go, and to know that once again they are as they began: alone, the one for the other. Children come to the marriage, but they are not intended to stay with the marriage. Whether we like it or not, they will leave. The couple is made to remain together. This is the divine plan, and this is the beauty of the relationship called marriage.

Some parents allow one of their children to sleep with them. Remember that the children will do anything to be able to sleep with their parents. If this is permitted, it should be for only a very short time. The couple should never stop sleeping together because there is not room for the three of them in the bed. The person that is one too many is the child. Don't let your son or daughter become used to sleeping in your bed. If the child is already doing that, move him or her out as quickly as possible. The marriage bed is for the couple. Burn that ship!

When the couple is not happy, the natural tendency is to take refuge in the person or persons who will give us affection, in this case, the children. This happens very frequently in our Latin culture. In the majority of cases, this is not expressed verbally, but one member of the couple—usually the mother—has an excessive emotional attachment to her children. She devotes her affection, care, and love to them, above what she should give to her husband.

We must maintain the order of priority in our family relations, without ceasing to love our children. The more the parents love one another, understand and respect each other, the more stability the children have in which to grow. This has nothing to do with the economic level of the family. The values of life, and for life, which form our character are learned at home. One of those principles is to demonstrate to our children the importance of the spouse in the marriage relationship. When they marry and establish their own home, they will have a worthy example to follow.
Someone once said that "our homes are factories where human beings are built, and there are some humans that leave the factory half built." What kind of human beings are you building in the factory that is your home? Every responsible couple must be concerned to equip their children the best that they can to be able to face a dysfunctional and hostile society.

Children are a blessing in the home, but they should never become a distraction which threatens the wholesome relationship of the parents. The home should never revolve around the children; it should revolve around the couple. The children are not the center of the home; the couple is. When this principle is not followed, the children are harmed. The children must not be ships of refuge for either one of the parents. We repeat, the children are lent to us, and we can enjoy them for a few years only. It is a law of life: they must go because it is not the divine plan that they remain forever with their parents.

I received an e-mail with an anonymous meditation called: "Our children as ships." Here are some sections of it:

> When we see a ship in port, we suppose that she is in her safest location, protected by a strong anchor. We know, however, that she is there preparing herself, being supplied and readied to be launched out to sea, to fulfill the destiny for which she was built, traveling to encounter her own adventures and risks.
>
> Our children are like that. They have their parents, comparable to the secure port, until they become independent. Notwithstanding all the security, protection, and provision that they receive from their parents, children are born to sail the seas of life, running their own risks and living their own adventures.... The safest place for the ship is the port, but it was not built to remain there.

The ship of friends

Another ship which must be burned is that of our friendships. What I am trying to say here is that every friendship of our life as a single person must be transferred to the list of friends of the couple. If any of these people cannot be part of the friends of the couple for any reason, that friendship must be burned or cut off. This does not mean that spouses cannot have friends, but always with the condition that these relationships do not compete with the marriage. Sometimes one of the spouses wants to continue his or her relations with friends as though he or she were still unmarried. These friendships do not involve the other spouse and take time away from the couple's time together. The married person must burn these ships.

I remember Tony (not his real name), who although having been married for six years, maintained a very close relationship with his former friends. They got together to drink and talk "man talk;" so women were not allowed. The tensions of his work and the difficulties in the home drew him more and more to this group, in which he attempted to forget his troubles. The advice he got from his friends led him to imitate their example, seeking what they called "release." Tony fell into infidelity, breaking his vows and endangering his home. Tony had rejected the very idea of infidelity, and was hostile to his friends who practiced it. But the pressure of the group that did not share his concern for his family led him to fall into it.

I also remember the case of a young couple with two children. The wife took a new job, and new friends with it. These were a group of divorced women with a very liberal lifestyle. The values of this group were very different from those that she and her husband had maintained during their eight years of marriage. She began to go out with her friends, to claim her space and the right to enjoy herself without her husband.

The husband came to me because he felt that he was losing his wife and his marriage. That inexperienced young woman began to turn from her husband for the life of a single woman that she had never known. Her circle of friends demanded more and more of her time. Again and again she came home with new ideas and new ways to experience the freedom that she thought she deserved. She would stay out all night drinking with her friends, visiting bachelorette clubs, enjoying life, as she described it. But these conditions did not last long. Not because the husband would not put up with them, but because she asked him for a divorce. She said she needed more freedom.

We must point out that not all groups of men or women act like that, but it is important that the friends of one spouse be friends of both. If the values of these friends are not those that you wish for your home, then it is preferable to burn these ships and build new friendships where both spouses are welcome. Life is full of small decisions. Each of them requires that we sacrifice something. Don't sacrifice your marriage. Certainly it is your best and greatest investment. Burn those ships.

The ship of previous relationships

It seems obvious that the previous relationships of the couple must be left behind, but this is not obvious in practice. Marriage should always be completely voluntary. To get married should be a free and enthusiastic decision that always must be accompanied by total abandonment of any other relationship. We give ourselves completely to receive the other person completely. Relationships from the past must remain there, in the past. We must not make comparisons or permit memories which will harm the health of our marriage.

There are too many cases in which apparently solid marriages have come apart because of the appearance of someone with whom one of the spouses previously had a romantic or some other type of relationship. In such cases we must not make even the slightest concession.

67

To do so may open a door which will be very hard to close. Those ships must be burned. When we do so, all chance of returning to the past disappears, and the destructive consequences of doing so as well.

By way of conclusion

The examples we have mentioned and compared to ships, cases that may have negative effects on the marriage, must be burned when they appear. As soon as the couple see that their family, their children, their friends or relationships from the past are occupying territory that belongs exclusively to the couple, they should act. And the spouse who is most closely connected to the situation must act first. In other words, if the problem is with my family or my friends, it's up to me to light the fire.

We are not saying in any way that our parents, children, friends, etc., are necessarily the cause of a divorce, but they can have a powerful influence in certain circumstances. Family and friends are, and always should be, a blessing that contributes to the stability and wholesome development of the marriage. But when they hinder the relationship of the couple, they become ships to be burned. There are obviously many other "ships" that can affect the couple and lead to divorce, but here we will limit ourselves to the ones mentioned.

When Naíme and I got married, God gave us the wisdom to make decisions from the beginning that would shape our married life permanently. One of those decisions was that we would never use the word divorce, not even as a joke. By that action we were declaring: *We are married for life, until death do us part.* We knew that this was an important decision, but we really did not understand how important it was until we began to help other couples who had crises in their marriages.

During our years as marriage counselors and speakers at events for married couples, we have had the opportunity to help many couples who were on the brink of divorce. They saw it as the only way to escape from their disagreements. And like the army of Hernán Cortés, faced with any threat, they would run to take refuge in their ships as though that would protect them, instead of facing the enemy with courage and resolution. Currently, many couples enter matrimony with a predisposition to divorce. It is very common to hear: *We are getting married, but if things don't work out, we'll get a divorce.* It is as though marriage were something as insignificant as buying an article of clothing, and returning it if it doesn't fit.

It is like keeping a card up one's sleeve, to use if necessary. And this attitude works against them or their union, because it diminishes their courage and commitment to risk everything and burn their ships, fighting for their marriage. This same attitude becomes the "ship" that they board to escape from reality to an uncertain future. They give up their dreams, their plans, their entire project of building a life together. Yes, yes, we do understand that in some cases, divorce is the lesser evil. But it always should be seen as an evil, which contrasts sharply with God's plan that marriage should work for a lifetime.

"Burning your ships" should be an act involving both partners. "Burning your ships" requires courage, resolution, and total commitment to the marriage. We give up one relationship to defend another. Yes, it is both a renunciation and a commitment. It unites these two actions: one which repels and another which attracts; one which rejects and the other which unites. In most cases in which divorce occurs, there is no longer the willingness to "burn the ships."

Sometimes couples give in to divorce, although they have not given up all hope for the marriage, because of pride, because they are very hurt, or because they think that there is no use in continuing the struggle, or that it is too late.

If great battles are fought for the purpose of winning a war or conquering a territory or gaining a crown, how much more should we fight to protect the most special, extraordinary relationship that we humans lay claim to, that is, marriage. It was only about this most special of relationships that Jesus said: So they are no longer two, but one. *Therefore what God has joined together, let man not separate.*[20] Therefore, fight without hesitation or reserve for your marriage, and burn those ships. All the power of God is at your disposal to enable you to do so.

---

20 Matthew 19:6, KJV

Discussion questions:

1. What does "burning your ships" mean with reference to your marriage?

2. What ships can you identify in your marriage that you should burn before they destroy your relationship?

3. Which is the ship that will cost you the most to burn? Explain.

4. Take a moment to talk with your spouse. Identify together each one of the ships that is affecting your marriage. Then make plans to hold a "ship-burning party," to clear the path that you will travel together in matrimony.

Chapter 4

Achilles' Heel
Weaknesses vs. Strengths

*"A chain is only as strong as
its weakest link" Thomas Reid.*

Achilles' Heel
Weaknesses vs. Strengths

Achilles was the most important Greek hero in the Trojan War. He was young, quick, passionate, and fundamentally warlike. He came out well in every battle, and distinguished himself as an untiring warrior. No one could harm him; he appeared to be immortal. This legend has its origin in the incomplete poem called Achilleid, written by Statius in the first century. It contains a version of the myth of the birth of Achilles that is not found in other sources. This account says that when Achilles was born, his mother Thetis attempted to give him immortality by dipping him in the River Styx. But she held him by the right heel in order to submerge him in the current of the river. For that reason that specific part of his body remained vulnerable; it was the only place where Achilles could be wounded in battle. So Achilles was invulnerable in his entire body, except in his heel.[21]

It was said that Troy could not be conquered without the help of Achilles. In fact, when he did not fight, the Trojans prevailed. Achilles killed Hector, the hero of Troy. He fought in many battles and killed the Amazon warrior Penthesilea. Finally Paris wounded Achilles with an arrow in his only vulnerable point, his heel. Achilles died from the wound. From then on, the expression "Achilles' heel" was used to indicate the weak point that every human being has.[22]

Although it is only a legend, what is most certainly true is that we all have a weak point that makes us vulnerable, more fragile, in situations that demand determination. An

---

[21] Wikipedia. Achilles' Heel. http://es.wikipedia.org/wiki/Talón_de_Aquiles.(July 12, 2013).

[22] Poesía.bligoo.com. Achilles. http://poesia.bligoo.com/content/view123488/Aquiles.html. (June 4, 2013).

inappropriate habit, lack of discipline, a bad example, disreputable thoughts or attitudes, or the tendency toward certain failings may point to gray areas in a person's character.

The education that we receive or that we impart far too often is deficient in character formation. We focus more on knowledge, on skills, on accumulated experience, rather than on strengthening the character of the person. In every area of human knowledge—schools, universities, institutes, seminaries, churches, or any other place of learning—we tend to concentrate more on the mind than on the heart of the learners. Sometimes the urgency of competition or programs, the demands of the market, and the pressure to obtain results make us forget that we are working with human lives. These people have relationships and interact with others in a complex world that demands more than mere intellectual knowledge, more than information, but rather strength of character. An Arab saying goes: *"Money lost is a small loss. Health lost is a greater loss. Character lost is everything lost."*

Speaking about ethics, John Maxwell mentioned the failures of the directors of great companies, who led their businesses and thousands of associates into bankruptcy. Maxwell said that these failures are nothing more than sad, shameful examples of failures of character. [23]

Similar things happen in the ecclesiastical world, where we see religious leaders fall suddenly. A little investigation will show that the name of the failure may vary, but the cause will always be the same: a serious character flaw (hidden sins). As a wise man said: *"You may rise to the top by your talents, but only your character (obedience to God) will keep you there."*

---

23 John Maxwell. Ethics 101: There's Only One Rule for Making Decisions. (First Warner Books Printing, 2003), 52

Our personal Achilles' heel

We cannot deny our surrounding nor our history and origins. We are the fruit of our life experiences. Each and every one of them has left some small mark upon us. They are like the blows of the hammer and chisel on the hard rock, that little by little have shaped the person that we are today. As Ortega Gasset expressed it: *"I am what I am plus my circumstances."* [24]

We all are an amalgam, with a range of virtues and strengths which we loudly proclaim and show off without criticism. But likewise we have our faults and weaknesses, which we normally hide and admit only in secret, perhaps. It's likely that we talk about some of the areas in which we are strong, and even give seminars about them, but we keep quiet about the places where we are weak. But there is one person in our life that sees both, the weaknesses as well as the strengths. That person is our spouse; we cannot hide them from him or her, and he or she also suffers because of them.

We need to identify our weaknesses, and go so far as to classify them. There are at least three reasons for identifying them.

1. To recognize that we have them. It is most helpful to accept that we have defects and weaknesses. The first thing that this does in our favor is to make us human. We recognize that we are part of a fallen race. Although we were created in the image of our perfect Maker, we have sinned, and therefore are classified as sinners. The Bible says: *There is no one righteous, not even one; there is no one who understands*, no

---

24 José Ortega y Gasset, Meditaciones del Quijote. (Madrid: Publicaciones de la Residencia de Estudiante, 1914), p. 43

Daniel Villa

one who seeks God. All have turned away, they have together become worthless; there is no one who does good, not even one....all have sinned and fall short of the glory of God.[25] By admitting that we all have our "Achilles heel," we are enabled to be more compassionate regarding the mistakes of others.

2. To present them to God, seeking forgiveness and help. We don't want to give the impression that weaknesses of temperament are synonymous with sin, but that they are the product of human sin. Our admission of our vulnerability and sinfulness should necessarily lead us to God, seeking His pardon and seeking His indispensable help. God, our loving Father, has promised to forgive us through His Son Jesus, giving us strength and tools to overcome. Besides this, with the presence of the Holy Spirit, we can change our attitudes. The Bible declares: Therefore, if anyone is in Christ, he is a new creation; the old has gone, the new has come![26] And this leads us to the third purpose.

3. To work on them. There would be little value in recognizing our faults and weaknesses if this did not move us to formulate a plan to strengthen them. We don't seek an admission of weakness in order to hide behind it with the argument that to err is human. The idea is to identify the weak areas of our temperament and character, in order to work to become a better person: to abandon bad habits and substitute better ones for them. Suppose that someone admits that he or she easily gets angry. This person can make a plan to better control his anger. For example: begin by asking divine help; admit or confess that he/she becomes irritable easily; make a list of things that make

25 Romans 3:10-12, 23
26 1 Corinthians 5:17

78

one angry; understand that anger is a response that has been learned or chosen in certain circumstances, and that he/she can choose to respond differently. One can learn other responses; he can even make a list of these responses and anticipate his attitude when these occasions arise. This is totally possible, and even more so since we can count on the help of the holy Comforter. What are your weak points? Notice that I said Yours, not those of your spouse. Dare to make a list of them and take control today of the gray areas of your personality.

The Achilles' heel in marriage

We bring to our marriage all that we are as persons. The act of getting married in itself has no power to change us, indeed that is not its purpose. With perhaps a few rare exceptions, the day after the wedding we will have the same values, points of view, ideas, and customs that we always had. All our history comes with us: our values from our home, life lessons learned, contributions from our studies, and influences that have shaped us. All this baggage of our life experience will accompany us into the marriage bed; some of this will strengthen that relationship, but some will weaken it. Each spouse will bring his or her knapsack of virtues and defects, strengths and weaknesses, wealth or scarcity, good and bad habits, successes and failures.

It is most helpful to recognize and accept that we have defects and weaknesses. One of our goals in pre-marriage counseling is that the couple recognize, accept, and work on both their weaknesses as well as their strengths. As a team, the couple needs to know what resources each member can contribute to the relationship, and how to use these to the best advantage. Moreover, knowing the weaknesses of each will help the other member to understand his or her behaviors and to have different attitudes.

I remember a woman who in a session of family counseling gave a marvelous description of her husband as someone: practical, self-sufficient, decisive, extroverted, not frightened by adversity. A man that recognizes opportunities and with mental agility and clarity can make quick decisions, set himself a goal, and achieve it easily. He is an organized person, intuitive, with great qualities as a leader. But  she could not understand why her husband, at the same time was hostile, cruel, sarcastic, insensitive, and stubborn. Besides being irritable, cold, and obstinate.

THE MARRIAGE TENDS TO BLESS THE COUPLE BY SUBTRACTING WEAKNESSES AND ADDING STRENGTHS.

The husband didn't want to be left behind, and with the help of informative material that I provided, he described his wife as: a perfectionist, self-controlled, talented, profoundly analytic, with an excellent mind, creative, with deep feelings, self-sacrificing, a faithful friend who would go so far as to make sacrifices for others if necessary. But at the same time he found a great collection of weaknesses, such as: negative, pessimistic, vindictive, fussy, depressed, and temperamental. And that is just how we are, full of extraordinary virtues y peppered with weaknesses and defects.

It is interesting that God has the habit of complementing us by giving us someone different from ourselves, one who will be strong in the areas in which we are weak. I can admit that I am slow to make decisions, but my wife makes them quickly. It is likely that the person whom you decided to marry is different from you. That is because opposites attract. A pessimist tends to marry an optimist; a reserved person with someone who loves to talk; the persistent person with someone laid back. So it is extremely valuable to know and manage both the strengths as well as the weaknesses, to make them work for the good of the marriage.

What are the strengths and weaknesses of your marriage? The strong points would be the individual strengths of each spouse, plus the sum of uniting these qualities. On the other hand, the weaknesses of the marriage are the result of subtracting the individual weaknesses from the individual strengths. Because, as we already said, the strengths of one tend to make up for the weaknesses of the other. So if we are wise in following the divine plan, we can enjoy the fact that marriage tends to bless the couple by subtracting weaknesses and adding strengths.

When we don't follow God's plan and allow our natural selfishness to rule, we tend to adopt attitudes that are harmful to the marriage:

1. We become experts in identifying and pointing out the weaknesses of our spouse.
2. We become blind to the strengths and virtues that he or she has.
3. At the same time, we become more indulgent and flexible regarding our own weaknesses, seeking all kinds of justification for them.
4. We come to the point of being irritated by the abilities that we formerly admired in the person we love, the same points that made us fall in love with him or her, the ones we were so eager to recognize.
5. Consciously or unconsciously, we try to make that special person who enchanted us more like ourselves.

The final result of this process is that we begin to see our spouse as our enemy. Our "better half" begins that chemical process by which it turns into "our bitter half." But remember, if my spouse is a bitter half, I am the other half. Instead of enjoying and taking advantage of the rich diversity that we obtain together, we become bitter and adopt critical attitudes. The Lord Jesus, revealing His understanding of human nature, said to some people who liked to judge and criticize:

Why do you look at the speck of sawdust in your brother's eye and pay no attention to the plank in your own eye? How can you say to your brother, "Let me take the speck out of your eye," when all the time there is a plank in your own eye? You hypocrite, first take the plank out of your own eye, and then you will see clearly to remove the speck from your brother's eye.[27]

But we should remember that the divine plan is to complement us with someone different from ourselves, and that we should unite strengths and subtract weaknesses. It is truly a blessing that marriage is only between two people.

It would be very valuable to know and manage both the strengths and weaknesses of your marriage. You might ask: "I understand the importance of knowing our strengths, but why bother about understanding our weaknesses? If someone has diabetes, should he know it? Of course! Not knowing about it does not stop the disease or slow it down. On the contrary, the patient runs a greater risk, because he does not take the precautions that a person with diabetes should follow. Exactly the same is true in marriage.

[27] Matthew 7:3-5, NIV

The following chart presents four personality types, identified as expressive, ambitious, calm, and thoughtful. It gives a list of the weaknesses and strengths of each type. I invite you to attempt to identify yourself based on your characteristics. When both members of the couple do this exercise, they realize that they are neither totally bad nor totally good. The most important fact is that each has both good and bad points. But the idea is not to hide behind our weaknesses, arguing that "to err is human," but rather to work on the marriage.

Expressive:		Ambitious:	
__Vivacious	__Forgetful	__Goal oriented	__Insensitive
__Playful	__Distracted	__Experienced	__Stressed
__Enthusiastic	__Unorganized	__Entrepreneur	__Manipulative
__Willing to please	__Impulsive	__Takes initiative	__Bossy
__Participating	__Not detail oriented	__Confident	__Opinionated
__Makes friends quickly	__Poor listener	__Determined	__Impatient
__Charismatic	__Follower	__Hard worker	__Intolerant of others' errors
__Spontaneous	__Naughty	__Effective administrator	__Difficult to say "sorry"
__Talkative	__Superficial relationships	__Decisive	__Critic
__Forgiving	__Risky	__Visionary	
Calm:		**Thoughtful:**	
__Enjoys peace	__Does not easily see own faults	__Sensitive	__Speaks ill of him/herself
__Composed	__Procrastinator	__Compassionate	__Does not value him/herself
__Establishes peace	__Slow to make difficult decisions	__Devoted to his/her few friends	__Perfectionist
__Diligent	__Avoids conflicts	__Organized	__Pessimist
__Good listener	__Engaging	__Works for no recognition	__Extremely detailed
__Cautious	__Indifferent with others	__Persistent	__Easily hurt
__Pleasant	__Too calm	__Creative	__Meditates too much on errors of the past
__Maintains composure	__Avoids difficult decisions	__Analytical	__Judgmental
__Even tempered	__Apathetic	__Sacrificed	__Easily worries
__Relaxed		__Appreciates beauty	__Easily feels guilty

[28]

Obviously, the weaknesses characteristic of a temperament do not have to be an indelible mark on the person. There are multiple factors that can affect a person and help him or her to develop different attitudes and improve or jettison the weaknesses particular to his temperament.

---

[28] Temperaments. http://www.slideshare.net/bjovencentral/temperamentos-4676006?nomobile=true (January 12, 2014).

There is a spiritual experience called "conversion." It happens when a person has received enough light to understand his spiritual condition, seeing his condition as a sinner, and this moves him to accept Jesus as his Savior and Lord. Through the work of the Holy Spirit, who comes to inhabit our spirit, Jesus transforms us from the inside out. The Bible declares that the fruit—that is, the result—of the presence of the Holy Spirit in us is: *love, joy, peace, patience, kindness, goodness, faithfulness, gentleness, and self-control.*[29]

Let us consider as an example the negative characteristics pointed out by the couple in the case we mentioned formerly. She found that he was hostile, cruel, sarcastic, insensitive, and stubborn. And also irritable, cold, and obstinate. He, on the other hand, said that she was negative, pessimistic, vindictive, fussy, depressed, and temperamental. Let's look at how the fruit of the Spirit in our life can help us to change these weaknesses.

His Weaknesses - Fruit of the Spirit - Her Weaknesses

His Weaknesses	Fruit of the Spirit	Her Weaknesses
Cruel ⟷	**Love** ⟷	Revengeful
Cold	**Joy (happiness)**	
Hostile	**Peace**	Negative
Irritable	**Patience**	Fussy
Insensitive	**Kindness**	Depressed
Sarcastic	**Goodness**	
	Faithfulness	Pessimist
Stubborn	**Gentleness (humility)**	
Obstinate	**Self-control**	Temperamental

The presence of the Holy Spirit helps us with each weakness. The Christian counselor Dr. Henry Brant once

---

[29] Galatians 6:22-23, NIV

said: "We can fall back on our background as an excuse for our behavior only until the moment that we receive Jesus Christ as our Lord and personal Savior. After that, we can count on a new inner power that enables us to change our conduct."[30]

We all have an Achilles heel. But like the hero of the legend, let it be only our heel, and let us work to improve that weakness. May our character be like a rock, and our relationship like a strong, unbreakable chain. May we build healthy, robust homes. May our greatest recommendation be our character. Our children expect this. Our society needs it. Our God demands it.

---

[30] Building a better world. Temperaments. http://nelmazuera.blogspot.com /2010_09_27_archive.html (January 12, 2014)

Questions for discussion:

1. Why is our character important in our marriage?

2. Which are the weakest links in the chain of your character, and why?

3. Why is it important to identify our weaknesses? What can we do about them to improve our marriage relationship?

4. What negative consequences are there when selfishness reigns in our marriage?

5. What is your Achilles heel? Do you try to submerge yourself in your River Styx to make yourself invulnerable in your marriage, without realizing that your heel is not covered?

Chapter 5

**An eye for an eye,
A tooth for a tooth**
A principle to disregard

"You have heard that it has been said: 'An eye for an eye and a tooth for a tooth.' But I say to you: Do not resist those that do you harm. If someone slaps you on the cheek, then turn and let him slap you on the other cheek too". Mathew 5:38 – 42, (NIV)

An eye for an eye, tooth for a tooth
A principle to disregard

These declarations Jesus made are a part of his teachings and are known as the Sermon on the Mount. Jesus cites the oldest law in the world: *"An eye for an eye and a tooth for a tooth."* This is known as the law of Talion.

The term law of Talion (Latin: lex tailonis) refers to a judicial principle of retributive justice in which the law imposes punishment based upon the crime committed. The term "Talion" is derived from the Latin word "talis" or "tale," that means the same or identical, which means not referring to an equivalent punishment but to an identical punishment.[31]   The retribution would not be more or less than that received. The retribution would be neither more nor less than the injury received. That is to say, if the aggressor injured his victim causing the loss of his left arm, he could not be executed for that offense, nor sentenced to lose an eye. The penalty for the aggressor would be the loss of his left arm. The best-known expression of the law of Talion is "an eye for an eye and a tooth for a tooth," as it appears in the Old Testament.

The law became an integral part of the ethics and justice in the Old Testament. When God spoke to Moses and the town giving the laws which would guide them, he also included this one. In Exodus 21:23-25 He says: *"But if there is serious injury, then you are to take life for life, eye for eye, tooth for tooth, hand for hand, foot for foot, burn for burn, wound for wound, bruise for bruise."* Leviticus 24:19-20 includes some of the words God gave to Moses to become laws for Israel: *"If anyone injures his*

---

[31] William Barclay, The Gospel of Matthew, Volume 1. (The Westminster Press: Philadelphia, 1975), 86

neighbor, whatever he has done must be done to him: fracture for fracture, eye for eye, tooth for tooth. As he has injured the other, so he is to be injured."
Deuteronomy 19:21 speaks of the punishment for a false witness, saying: *"Show no pity: life for life, eye for eye, tooth for tooth, hand for hand, foot for foot."*

The commentator William Barclay clarifies the lex Talionis, was not, as it was believed, a bloody and savage legislation, and it was instead a code filled with mercy. Its purpose was to limit personal vengeance. When a member of a tribe caused harm to another member of another tribe the victim's tribe members would arise and drag that person and it was a normal occurrence. Before that law was established, punishment was imposed to the person causing the harm as long as the damage was intentional. An eye for an eye, a tooth for a tooth and a foot for a foot. This law seeked to eliminate the abuse and killing of innocent people. [32]

Deuteronomy 19:18 was not a law that gave the individual the right to vengeance; it was a law stipulating the punishment by judge and jury. The Talion law was not administered by the individual but by a judge's verdict.

This law is the bases for the popular and million dollar lawsuits of today. This is because rarely was the law applied as it was written. Obviously, payment of a good eye as well as that of a good tooth for a bad eye or bad tooth was to the Jewish judges not applying this law. It would literally be doing the opposite of doing justice. Very quickly were damages compensated with money.
It is important to clarify that the ethics of life and the justice of the Old Testament was much broader than that

---

[32] Barclay, p. 86.

law and was never limited to it.

Barclay states:
> We have to remember that lex Talionis is not the total ethics of the Old Testament. *Do not seek revenge or bear a grudge against one of your people, but love your neighbor as yourself. I am the Lord (Leviticus 19:18). Do not say, "I'll pay you back for this wrong!" Wait for the Lord, and he will deliver you (Proverbs 20:22). Do not say, "I'll do to him as he has done to me; I'll pay that man back for what he did" (Proverbs 24:29).*[33]

Nevertheless, the Pharisees appealed to this law to justify retribution and personal vengeance. They quoted this commandment with the purpose of defeating its purpose. They said that God Himself had given them the right to exact vengeance. So they would use the law given to prevent vengeance in order to avenge themselves.

In one section of the Sermon on the Mount Jesus told His hearers: *You have heard that it was said, "Eye for eye, and tooth for tooth." But I tell you....*[34] In doing this, Jesus is reinterpreting the law in order to teach the people its original, true intention. Jesus rejects the interpretation of the Pharisees of this ancient principle, and introduces not only the principle of non-vengeance but also that of brotherly love. The idea of offering *the other cheek* is not to give in to provocation. It means to overcome the desire to return the insult, to defend one's honor, to return the offense. Non-vengeance is also to reject anger and resentment.

[33] Ibid.
[34] Matthew 5:38-39, KJV.

The law of Talion and your marriage

If a couple were to try to apply this law in their marriage, they would end up blind and toothless. Although this law was abolished by Jesus in the New Testament, or replaced by the law of love, today we still see this kind of behavior in the daily life of people, and even worse, in the daily life of married couples and families that make up our communities of faith.

Every couple that aspires to have peace in their home and to keep it for a long time, that is, until death separates them, must eradicate from their married life any action motivated by vengeance and the spirit of retribution. Intentionally and firmly we must resist the "natural" tendency to make the other party pay for what they did to us. The offended spouse tends to "repay with the same coin."

In most cases the reaction is instinctive, not planned. The response is an action as great as or greater than the one received. Spouses often say: "If she doesn't speak to me, I don't speak to her. If he yells at me, I yell at him." Communication will be broken, and probably neither one will know how the problem began. Because we assume that the initial behavior was directed against us, and we don't take the time to investigate the reason for the other's attitude, which we would do with a friend. Here is an extensive definition of vengeance:

> Vengeance consists primarily in the revenge against a person or group in response to a bad action received. Although many aspects of revenge resemble the concept of justice, revenge generally pursues a goal that is more offensive. The desire of revenge consists in forcing a person who has done something bad to suffer the same

pain that he inflicted, or it is done to make sure that the person or group will not commit such damage again. Revenge is an act that, in the majority of cases, causes pleasure to the person who did it, because of the feeling of bitterness that it causes the antecedent.[35]

There is no doubt that misunderstandings and tensions in the daily relations of the couple are more common than we would like to admit. Arguments and disagreements tend to show up in married life, and one must make the necessary adjustments. But the main goal is not that there be no conflicts, but to face them wisely. Conflict has the potential to strengthen the couple when it is managed constructively. Frequently there will be something to forgive. We must decide whether we will let go of anger and forgive, or if we will retain the resentment and allow it to turn into bitterness, which will produce vengeance. We must forgive. It is essential to forgive in love. The Bible teaches: *"Hatred stirs up dissension, but love covers over all wrongs."*[36] It also says: *"Above all, love each other deeply, because love covers over a multitude of sins."*[37]

We must clarify that when we talk about common conflicts within the relations of the couple, in no way do we include situations like mistreatment or abuse in any of its forms (domestic violence). Nor do we include marital infidelity or irresponsibility in assuming our proper role. We ought not to accept such situations or others similar to them as "common events" in marriage. Although the commandment prohibiting vengeance covers all situations, in such cases it is necessary to seek help immediately and try to resolve them.

Another fault committed by a spouse that provokes

---

[35] Wikipedia. Revenge. http://es.wikipedia.org/wiki/Venganza. (January 15, 2013).
[36] Proverbs 10:12 NIV
[37] 1 Peter 4:8, NIV.

vengeance by what we call "the innocent party" is adultery. In these cases vengeance is more carefully considered, more planned. Although there is full awareness of what the process implies, the rage and pain do not allow the sufferer to see any more intelligent solution, but only to think: "I want him/her to feel what I feel." Others also consider doing physical harm to their spouse.

Vengeance brings very grave consequences. There are many people behind bars today, and many others in cemeteries because people allowed to mature, first in their mind and then in their heart, a vengeance that finally produced fatal results. It is exactly against this attitude that the apostle Paul speaks in Romans 12:17-21:

Do not repay anyone evil for evil. Be careful to do what is right in the eyes of everybody. If it is possible, as far as it depends on you, live at peace with everyone. Do not take revenge, my friends, but leave room for God's wrath, for it is written: "It is mine to avenge; I will repay," says the Lord. On the contrary: "If your enemy is hungry, feed him; if he is thirsty, give him something to drink. In doing this, you will heap burning coals on his head." Do not be overcome by evil, but overcome evil with good.

Paul begins by saying that we should not repay anyone evil for evil. We should not allow ourselves to be motivated by the desire for vengeance. That we should not attempt to collect from anyone, in this case our spouse, for some fault committed against us. Paul says: Do not repay; that is, "don't get upset, don't be moved by passion, don't repay with the same coin." And this brings us to the last part of the text: Do not be overcome by evil, but overcome evil with good. We must not allow the evil done to us to take control of us. We must not allow the evil desire for vengeance to dominate our feelings—just the opposite. We will overcome this unwholesome desire and we will do good, even though we received evil. In these words we find guidance about how to act with an enemy. But in our case we are not dealing with an enemy, but rather with the person we love and with whom we are one flesh. To injure that person is to injure ourselves. If what Paul teaches is true regarding an enemy, how much more in relation to our spouse. Perhaps this is a good time to remember that our spouse is not our enemy. Let's say "No" to vengeance, as expressed in this poem by José Martí:

> *I cultivate a white rose*
> *in July or in January*
> *to give to my dear friend*
> *who extends her/his sincere hand.*
>
> *And to that cruel one who rips*
> *the heart that keeps me alive*
> *neither thorns nor nettles do I send*
> *I cultivate a white rose.*[38]

The sad and frightening scene we observe in society at large is the direct result of the conditions in our homes. Because of the absence of love, respect, and understanding, abuse, infidelity, and divorce have proliferated. It could be called the reign of sin. When speaking of our human condition without God, Jesus said: *For from within, out of men's hearts, come evil thoughts, sexual immorality, theft, murder, adultery, greed, malice, deceit, lewdness, envy, slander, arrogance and folly.*[39]

Sin not only separates us from God and condemns us for eternity, but it also makes us live miserable lives.

---

[38] Poemas del alma. I cultivate a white rose. http://www.poemas-del-alma.com/jose-marti-cultivo-una- rosa-blanca.htm (January 12, 2013).

[39] Mark 7:21-23, NVI.

But Jesus has come to give us life, and give it to us in abundance. We need to go to Him, begging Him to forgive our sins and give us the gift of eternal life, and the resources to live an abundant life. Our society needs men and women who genuinely live out the Word of God, and homes built upon the values and teachings of the Bible.

An anonymous couplet goes: "Whoever forgives when he could avenge, is very close to being saved." This makes me think of the Biblical story of Joseph forgiving his brothers. The account begins in Genesis chapter 37. When Joseph was a young man about 17 years old, ten of his brothers conspired to sell him as a slave. This decision was motivated by jealousy, since Joseph was the favorite of his father. The old man was told that his son had been devoured by a wild animal. Young Joseph's odyssey continued for thirteen long years.

He first served as a slave in the household of a high-ranking Egyptian military officer. There, although he performed excellent service, he was falsely accused and thrown into jail and forgotten. Later, God miraculously delivered him from prison and elevated him to the position of second-in-command in the kingdom. And it was from that elevated position in the greatest world power of the day that he met with his ten brothers, who knelt before him without recognizing him. At this point Joseph had the power and authority to kill them if he had so chosen. What would you have done? These were Joseph's words: *"And now, do not be distressed and do not be angry with yourselves for selling me here, because it was to save lives that God sent me ahead of you." Joseph said to them, "Don't be afraid. Am I in the place of God? You intended to*

GOD WILL USE EVEN THE WICKEDNESS OF THOSE WHO WANT TO HARM US TO BRING US BLESSINGS.

harm me, but God intended it for good to accomplish what is now being done, the saving of many lives." [40]

What an incredible attitude! Joseph showed that he knew who he was and who his God was. I believe that God will use even the wickedness of those who want to harm us to bring us blessing. Like Joseph, let us focus on God's overall plan, not on some of His instruments. Let us never raise our hand to avenge ourselves. We have a God who does that for us.

We conclude by quoting a variety of sayings about vengeance. We do not necessarily agree one hundred per cent with every word, but even so, they give us food for thought.

1. "It is not possible to avenge a crime without committing another." Borel d'Hauterive.
2. "An act of justice allows us to close a chapter; an act of violence will write another chapter." Marilyn vos Savant.
3. "A true way to revenge with an enemy is not to show up." Marco Aurelio.
4. "Certainly, in taking revenge, a man is but even with his enemy; but in passing it over, he is superior." Sir Francis Bacon.
5. "A man who wants revenge, keeps his own wounds open, which otherwise would heal, and do well." Sir Francis Bacon.
6. "Revenge is a pleasure that only lasts one day; generosity is a sentiment that will make you happy eternally." Rosa Luxemburg.
7. "The insult only hurts when we remember it; the best revenge is forgetting." Harold Hard Crane

---

[40] Genesis 45:5; 50:19-20, NIV.

8. "We never feel well by having practiced evil. Resentment and revenge never provide happiness." Luis de Argote y Gongora

9. "Revenge is sweet only to those whose rancor has distorted their taste." Jaime Tenorio Valenzuela

10. "The cruelest revenge is the scorn of any possible revenge." Johann Wolfgan Goethe

11. "When one is thirsty for revenge one is hungry of more."   Anonymous

12. "Revenge, the sweetest morsel to the mouth that ever was cooked in hell." Walter Scott[41]

---

[41] Sabiduría.com. Revenge. http://www.sabidurias.com/result_tag.php?palabra=venganza&lang=es&tag= 1840&_pagi_pg=2 (February 6, 2012)

Questions for discussion:

1. With what principle or commandment does Jesus replace the law of talion? Explain your opinion about this.

2. In your marriage, do you consider as "normal" certain situations like mistreatment, domestic abuse, infidelity, or irresponsibility in general? Why?

3. What is vengeance, and what harm does it produce in marriage?

4. What would you do if you felt the desire to take vengeance on your spouse for something that he or she did to you?

Chapter 6

Siren Songs:
Say No to infidelity

*For the lips of the adulterous woman
drip honey, and her speech
is smoother than oil;
Proverbs 5:3 (NIV)*

The Songs of the Sirens
No to infidelity

It was Homer, in his book "The Odyssey," who made the first known reference to the mythological being called sirens. They were different from the concept that our culture has about that mythology. Those earliest references describe the sirens as monstrous birds with the face and breast of a woman that would devour their prey after attracting them by their terrible, bewitching and irresistible songs. Today they are imagined to be beautiful young women with the body of a fish. One author notes that this is the reason that some languages distinguish between the original or classical siren (German: Sirene) and the mermaid (German: Meerjungfrau).[42]

The expression "siren song" comes from the legend told by Homer about the hero Ulysses. When returning from the Trojan War, Ulysses knew that his ship would have to pass close to the island of the sirens. These beings were known and feared, because their melodious and irresistible songs would cause the sailors to throw themselves into the sea to reach them. The ships would be wrecked upon the reefs. Any survivors were cruelly murdered.

The astute Greek hero Ulysses was aware of the danger awaiting him, but desired to hear for himself those songs, so famous and feared. He devised a strategy that would allow him to hear them, and yet save his ship and companions. He ordered his men to stop their ears with wax to make them deaf to the terrible songs. Then he

---

[42] Wikipedia. Sirens. http://es.wikipedia.org/wiki/Sirena. (September 4, 2013).

103

Daniel Villa

requested that he be firmly tied to the main mast of the ship. In this way he could satisfy his curiosity to hear the songs of the sirens without yielding to their enchantments.

This song turns out to be melodious and heart-breaking, charged with beautiful promises. Ulysses shouts to his companions to release him, but of course they are deaf to his entreaties. At last the ship passes by and the heroes escape the deadly fate suffered by so many other sailors.

But Ulysses was not the only one to meet the sirens. The mythic poet Orpheus, who accompanied Jason in his search for the Golden Fleece, also was able to resist their fatal charms. At the instant when Jason and his men, the Argonauts, attracted by the beautiful voices, change course and go toward the dangerous reefs of the island, Orpheus takes his lyre and plays a song so sublime that it overwhelms the melodies of the sirens and saves the sailors from the deadly attraction.

The siren represents, among other things, that attraction toward perdition. Not in vain is it a creature that uses deceit to attract navigators to the coast, to later devour them. In colloquial language, "to hear siren songs" is synonymous with being bewitched. So we have the saying, "Sometimes you hear the song of a siren and you meet a sea lion."[43]

The myth of the sirens becomes a compendium of the dangers that await the couple and become stumbling blocks in the journey of their married life. But in particular we refer to infidelity. The song of the siren could represent immediate, easy pleasure, allowing oneself to be carried

[43]Animal Consciousness Cantos de sirena. (www.concienciaanimal.cl/paginas/temas/impri mirtemas.php?d=500) (December 17, 2013).

104

away by feelings and emotions. It is to give in to the tempting call of an affair full of passion that overwhelms the senses and does not consider consequences until it is too late. Through your reading, come aboard the ship that will take us to see up close those dangerous paths. Let's enter the "fascinating" world of "the sirens," and let us be ready to recognize their deceitful songs.

We begin with an interesting Biblical narrative that tells the story of an act of infidelity. A gullible youth was exposed to the danger and heard the song of the siren, and he believed every word he heard. At the very time that he was hastening to the arms of death, he thought himself to be the most fortunate man on the planet. Here is the story:

> At the window of my house I looked out through the lattice. I saw among the simple, I noticed among the young men, a youth who lacked judgment. He was going down the street near her corner, walking along in the direction of her house at twilight, as the day was fading, as the dark of night set in.
>
> Then out came a woman to meet him, dressed like a prostitute and with crafty intent. She took hold of him and kissed him and with a brazen face she said: "I have fellowship offerings at home; today I fulfilled my vows. So I came out to meet you; I looked for you and have found you! I have covered my bed with colored linens from Egypt. I have perfumed my bed with myrrh, aloes and cinnamon. Come, let's drink deep of love till morning; let's enjoy ourselves with love! My husband is not at home; he has gone on a long journey. He took his purse filled with money and will not be home till full moon." With persuasive words she led him astray; she seduced him with

105

her smooth talk. All at once he followed her like an ox going to the slaughter, like a deer stepping into a noose till an arrow pierces his liver, like a bird darting into a snare, little knowing it will cost him his life.

Now then, my sons, listen to me; pay attention to what I say. Do not let your heart turn to her ways or stray into her paths. Many are the victims she has brought down; her slain are a mighty throng. Her house is a highway to the grave, leading down to the chambers of death.[44]

The Island of the Sirens

This passage illustrates how a man or a woman can be seduced or can seduce with flattering words, similar to the song of the sirens. The infidelity narrated here reveals decisions or actions that people take in a given moment, which make it easy for them to fall into the trap of infidelity. Let's examine them:

To approach the island of the sirens: to expose oneself to temptation.

Some men commit adultery visiting brothels. In such cases, from the moment the man starts out for the brothel, he goes with the full intention of being with a woman who sells her body. No one would say, *"Oh, I went there but I didn't intend to have sex with a woman; I was just out for a walk."* And if he said that, no one would believe him.

But to approach the island of the sirens means to flirt with danger. It means to expose oneself to dangerous situations without necessarily having the intent, or a clear

[44] Esteban 2008. Siren Songs (Siren Songs). (www.esteban2008.wordpress.com /2008/02/29/los-cantos-de-sirena/) (December 17, 2013).

decision to commit adultery. There is a certain excitement in playing with danger, taking some risks by circling the temptation, and then withdrawing. The initial intention may be to approach a little, with the mistaken idea that one is in control and can stop at any time. But we must realize that even to flirt is too risky, and that many have not been able to retreat in time or in safety. Approaching the island of the sirens is like entering a minefield. Once inside, what had appeared to be a game is no longer a game, and the danger is imminent.

The young man of the story from Proverbs was walking toward the house of the woman. Let's suppose that he only intended to see whether she was outside the house, to see her from a distance. But "he was not counting on her cunning," (as a Hispanic superhero would say). She saw him, and with evil intent went out to meet him.

Another factor that increased the danger was that night was falling. Darkness was an ally of indiscretion. We see that he had approached a high-risk zone. As we already said, this gullible fellow was seeking an adventure, but possibly did not plan or expect it to reach the level that it did. The problem was that he exposed himself too much in a dangerous game, because the woman, using all her cunning, seduced him. In truth, we don't see that he offered much resistance. The fact was that *"he went to hear the song of the siren, but he was met by a sea lion."*

There are dangers that can be avoided with good judgment. Just as a recovering alcoholic avoids passing by certain places or meeting with his former drinking buddies, every prudent man or woman will avoid situations that will expose him or her to unnecessary dangers. One such situation occurs when a person who is married has a confidant of the opposite sex. This is an unnecessary risk. Such a confidential position should be filled by one's spouse, or a professional counselor or spiritual leader. If a confidant is needed, one should seek a reliable person of the same sex. Or another married couple could do very well in this capacity, a couple with sufficient maturity to be an example and help in one's married life.

It is wise to take simple measures at work that send the clear message that you are married and respect your spouse: things like always wearing your wedding ring, or keeping a Bible on your desk, which gives a clear message about your values. Also keep visible a photo of your spouse or your family, when possible. Don't talk about problems of the home. These should never be the topic of meal-time conversation; save them for talks with your counselor or confidant. Refuse openly and firmly any sexual insinuation, no matter how small it may appear. Do not participate in conversations of a sexual nature, or that may lead to sexual comments. Affirm your values openly and fearlessly.

We live in a society with a crisis of values, with double standards. This is deeper than a moral crisis, in which we know what is right and choose to do the wrong. The crisis of values is moral confusion, in which everything appears to be admissible. Everything bad has some good in it, and everything good has some bad. The motto is: Live and let live.[45] We should not feel uncomfortable or ashamed about stating that we have a code of values and that we live by them. Perhaps your companions will make fun of you, but inwardly they will feel admiration and respect. They may never tell you, but in the depths of their heart they would wish to be like you.

---

[45] Carlos Cuauhtémoc Sánchez. *Código de honor* (Code of honor). Audio book (Chicago: Giron Books, 2004).

To delight in the siren songs: Flattery, praise, adulation.

In the same way that the sirens could seduce with their songs, the woman in the story related by Proverbs used much flattery and praise, with words loaded with sensuality, to cause the young man to fall into her web. The story tells us that she saw him from her window and went out to meet him. But she tells him, "I came out of my house on purpose to look for you, and I found you!" She was making him believe that she needed to see him, that he was very important to her, and that she went out to look for him. When he heard her he thought, "Wow! She was looking for me. There are lots of other men, but she preferred me. She's really interested in me!" Poor naive fool! He easily fell for the clear invitation that she brazenly gave him—to take advantage of the absence of her husband for them to go to bed together. He paid attention to her words, and allowed himself to be convinced and seduced by her wiles.

Be careful of those voices that invite us to infidelity, and that paint a picture of a fabulous adventure that no one will ever know about. A good example of this is the song by Lolita Flores, entitled "Who is going to know?" (¿Quién lo va a saber?). Some of its verses read:

> Who is going to know
> if I keep you in my mind?
> Who can get between us?
> Who is going to know
> if I see you in my dreams?
> Who can know my dreams? Who?

> Who is going to know
> if you give me your lips
> and I give you my flower?

Who is going to know
if you don't say my name?
Who could suspect?

Who is going to know
if you hold me in your arms
and you press your skin to mine?
Who is going to know,
since the fields never talk?
Tell me, who is going to know?[46]

If a voice like this has sounded in your ears, understand that it is the song of a siren. Because people will find out! And even if they don't, God knows. We should tell Lolita that God does know. And He does not leave the guilty unpunished. Yes, my friend, we always reap what we sow.

So it is important not to overlook even slight actions or attitudes, such as a look that indicates a certain interest, or the slight but intentional physical contact, or seeking to spend time together, especially alone—these are clear signs of danger. As soon as they are detected, it is mandatory that one put a stop to the friendship with that man or woman, as the case may be.

We have helped both men and women recovering from an infidelity. Curiously, they never thought that they would fail their spouse in that way, but they did not take care in such simple matters as those we have mentioned. When the great majority of them realized that they were crossing the line, that the friendship was getting out of control, instead of cutting off the friendship, they began to seek excuses and reasons why they were incapable of remaining true to their spouse.

[46] Álbum, canción y letra. ¿Quién lo va a saber? http://www.albumcancionyletra.com/quien-lo-va-a-saber_de_lolita-flores_91542.aspx (November 4, 2013).

Some of them brazenly accused their spouse of responsibility for their unfaithfulness. This is typical. When we are lulled to sleep by the songs of a siren, we tend to rationalize our situation and seek excuses for the attitude we have taken. In his book *Be Careful of the Iceberg*, Bob Record says that for those who are falling into the trap of infidelity, the most common excuses are: *"I can manage this; I won't let anything get out of control." "God wants me to be happy." "I don't want anybody to get hurt." "The problem is that you don't understand my situation."*[47] Might this be your case?

Easy Prey (The Fall)

Once a man or woman has travelled blindly through the two steps mentioned above, he or she will become easy prey to infidelity. Upon arriving at this point, few men or women can resist the temptation. At first they think that they have control of the situation, but they soon realize that the seductive power of those siren voices is much stronger than they imagined. But it is not just a matter of strength, because to tell the truth, in reality it was not a struggle. They were not taking into consideration that the forbidden nectar was drugging their senses. Although reason was still shouting, "Wait! Stop!" its voice, which was already weak, was drowned out by the melodious, irresistible, bewitching songs of the passion of the moment. When the heart beats faster, reason is silenced, and passion reigns, stopping at nothing.

In the story which Proverbs relates we read: *"With persuasive words she led him astray; she seduced him with her smooth talk. All at once he followed her like an ox going to the slaughter, like a deer stepping into a*

---

[47] Bob Record, Beneath the Surface. Nashville: B&H Publishing Group, 2002. p. 28.

111

noose till an arrow pierces his liver, like a bird darting into a snare, little knowing it will cost him his life."

It is true that the sweetness of the moment may last for hours or days, weeks or months, but the dream will end, and will always collect its heavy price.

Infidelity affects the relationship of the couple deeply. Infidelity brings lack of trust, pain, emotional separation, and in many cases the complete breakdown of the relationship. Not only is the couple affected, but also the complete family. The children are caught between the conflicting decisions of their parents and are dragged into profound depths of depression. They suffer enormously as they see their world fractured, with no ability to repair it. We know of many cases where the couple is deeply pained by their error and repentant, wishing to go back in time and never commit the offense. It is not "till an arrow pierces his liver" that they can see the cost of their infidelity.

Avoid becoming a statistic

Cases abound of well-known people who lost everything: honor, position or ministry, and in some cases even their family, when, having been seduced by these siren songs that we have mentioned, they cast themselves into the tempting arms of infidelity. At the beginning, everything seemed like a game, a diversion, something that, although it had to be kept secret, did not have the power to cause major damage. Yes, everything appeared to be totally controllable, while at the same time attractive and seductive. Some of these folks said to themselves, I am only going to flirt a little; I know that I will never cross over the line.

Recent history records names like Jim Bakker, director of the PTL Club, who became involved in a sexual scandal with his secretary, and in a financial scandal which took him to prison. Bakker later wrote a book, "I Was Wrong."[48]

Another case very close to the evangelicals of the US was the fall of the well-known televangelist Jimmy Swaggart. More than eight million people per week watched Swaggart's programs around the world. In front of his congregation of over 7,000 people, as well as the TV audience, he was forced to confess that he had sinned. According to the press reports, another pastor, whom Swaggart had denounced for similar conduct, had decided to make public photographs of Swaggart with a prostitute. Swaggart saw his testimony, his ministry, and his influence destroyed because he did not learn from the similar case of the other pastor that he had denounced.[49]

We do not mention these cases to throw mud on those involved. Rather, we want to call the attention of the reader to them, to listen to this warning which shouts: Look at these men! Let their pain and brokenness be a warning to us not to commit their same errors and sins! Because as the saying goes: A wise person learns from the mistakes of others.

I have in my possession a photo of the ex governor of the State of New York, Eliot Spitzer, who lost his position and his reputation of an honest man when his relationship with a prostitute was uncovered. His expression in the picture indicates frustration, pain, impotence, remorse. Here are some of the things Spitzer said, according to the press report:

---

[48] The New York Times. Jim Bakker. http://www.nytimes.com/1987/03/21/us/bakker-evangelist-resigns-his-minstry-over-sexualincident.html (February 2, 2012).

[49] Rapture ready.com. The who's who? http://www.raptureready.com/twho/Jimmy_Swaggart.html (February 6, 2012).

In the past few days, I have begun to atone for my private failings with my wife Silda, my children, and my entire family. The remorse I feel will always be with me. Words cannot describe how grateful I am for the love and compassion they have shown me. From those to whom much is given, much is expected. I have been given much -- the love of my family, the faith and trust of the people of New York, and the chance to lead this state. I am deeply sorry that I did not live up to what was expected of me. To every New Yorker — and to all those who believed in what I tried to stand for — I sincerely apologize. [50]

It is painful to see what happened. We should see ourselves in his example and learn the lesson, remaining faithful to the principles that we preach. As we have already said, infidelity brings with it pain far beyond anything we can imagine, and an uncontrollable desire to turn back the clock and correct the error. Our inability to accomplish this increases our anguish and despair. And as though dealing with a conspiracy, our mind replays the failure again and again.

It is interesting to note that the Bible warns us about this. It raises its voice, attempting to catch our attention and save us from this suffering. In Proverbs chapter 5 we read things like:

"May you rejoice in the wife of your youth." "Keep to a path far from her (the adulterous woman), do not go near the door of her house, lest you give your best strength to others and your years to one who is cruel, and your toil enrich another man's house. At the end of your life

---

[50] Huffingtonpost.com. http://www.huffingtonpost.com/2008/03/12/spitzers-resignation-spee_n_91157.html. (January 2, 2012).

you will groan, when your flesh and body are spent. You will say, 'How I hated discipline! How my heart spurned correction!'"

Is this not the reality of those who have seen others occupy their privileged positions, for whom all that remains is the bitterness, the anguish, and that sour taste, "I knew this would happen?"

Let us remember a well-known case from the royal family of Israel. It is the story of David, the son of Jesse, the second king to occupy the throne of Israel and the most famous of them all. He was also known as "the sweet psalmist of Israel."[51] David had seven wives and many concubines when he met Bathsheba. This makes me think that the call to faithfulness is not a matter of number, but of the heart. David sinned gravely when he arranged for the death of one of his faithful soldiers in order to take his wife. It is remarkable the way in which God, through the prophet Nathan, brings David to an awareness of his sin. Let us read:

> The Lord sent Nathan to David. When he came to him, he said, "There were two men in a certain town, one rich and the other poor. The rich man had a very large number of sheep and cattle, but the poor man had nothing except one little ewe lamb he had bought. He raised it, and it grew up with him and his children. It shared his food, drank from his cup and even slept in his arms. It was like a daughter to him.
> "Now a traveler came to the rich man, but the rich man refrained from taking one of his own sheep or cattle to prepare a meal for the traveler who had come to him. Instead, he took the ewe lamb

---

[51] 2 Samuel 23:1, KJV

that belonged to the poor man and prepared it for the one who had come to him." David burned with anger against the man and said to Nathan, "As surely as the Lord lives, the man who did this deserves to die! He must pay for that lamb four times over, because he did such a thing and had no pity." Then Nathan said to David, "You are the man!" ...." Now, therefore, the sword will never depart from your house, because you despised me and took the wife of Uriah the Hittite to be your own.'" "This is what the Lord says: 'Out of your own household I am going to bring calamity upon you. Before your very eyes I will take your wives and give them to one who is close to you, and he will lie with your wives in broad daylight, before all Israel'".[52]

We must remember that David repented of his sin, but its consequences were severe. David paid for his sin many times over. The child of that adulterous union died. His family suffered great evils. The sword did plague his house. David's son Amnon raped his sister Tamar. Absalom, another son of David, killed his half-brother Amnon, and also rose up against his father David and attempted to seize the kingdom. In broad daylight, before the people, he possessed the wives of David. The kingdom would be divided, and his sons, the heirs to the throne, would not retain it. Many, many tears, and much shed blood were the price of that sin. That act performed in darkness God brought to light. We should remember that there is nothing hidden that will not be revealed. Sexual failures are not accidents. Even in unplanned cases, if there is a failure, it is due to

SEXUAL FAILURES ARE NOT ACCIDENTS.

[52] 2 Samuel 12:1-12 KJV

116

a weakening of the moral fiber of those involved.

Normally, there are warning signs that we are in a situation that is dangerous, or potentially dangerous. The individual begins to allow sexual thoughts regarding another person. Perhaps at first he may resist them, but this resistance becomes weaker and weaker, until at last these thoughts are continuous, and ever more daring and explicit.

Glances at persons of the opposite sex become more frequent and daring. The individual seeks sexual or pornographic material that perhaps he previously rejected. At this point he is looking for any kind of reasoning that will justify his intended action, in order to quiet his conscience. But the wise man or prudent woman will choose to strenuously reject immediate, easy, short-term pleasure, and will choose to strengthen this union with his or her spouse, seeking to improve that relationship. Remember, all the power of God is available to you to make your relationship work.

We conclude this chapter with a poem we wrote as we observed a person, who like the mythological Ulysses, was risking his life by flirting with the sweet, irresistible songs of sirens. The title of the poem is "Little Butterfly." May it not describe your case!

> *Little butterfly with golden wings,*
> *please don't approach so near the flame.*
> *There is danger to your wings so golden;*
> *Please don't approach the burning flame.*

And the butterfly with golden wings excitedly replied:

117

The flame is so intense and brilliant;
it enchants me and calls to me by name.
I know that danger lies in drawing near it,
but I must revel in the splendor of the

Little butterfly with golden wings,
You know the danger in the flame.
What would you be without your wings so lovely?
Keep back, little butterfly, far from the flame!

But the butterfly with golden wings replied:

Its shapes and colors are what attract me,
that delicious feeling of flirting with the flame.
I know there is danger in drawing near the burning,
but because I am in love I seek the flame!

Oh, little butterfly with golden wings,
you have embraced that all-consuming flame;
By its sparkling shapes you have been conquered.
.Your wings are gone; you will never be the same.

Questions for discussion:

1. For you, what constitutes a siren song? Mention one in particular that has aroused your interest during your matrimonial journey, and tell what you did to avoid falling into its trap.

2. What actions make it easy for you to fall into the trap of the siren song? How can you avoid them?

3. Do you freely approach the island of the sirens to listen to their songs and to prove that you will not yield to them?

4. Can you identify the siren songs in your workplace, your school, or even in your church? What will you do to be firm and reject them, even if you have to face them directly?

5. Based on the cases mentioned in this chapter, would you be willing to take the risk of personal experimentation, like the young man of Proverbs that we studied? Or would you choose to learn from the examples of others who fell, to be sure of victory?

Chapter 7

The Golden Rule
Diamond-quality conduct

*So in everything, do to others what you would
have them do to you, for this sums up the Law
and the Prophets. Matthew 7:12 (NIV)*

The Golden Rule
Diamond-quality conduct

To conclude these thoughts, we have chosen to refer to the famous Golden Rule. This is part of Jesus' teachings in what is known as the Sermon on the Mount. In the opinion of some scholars, this sermon is the most well-known of all the teachings of Jesus. One writer says: *"This is probably the most universally famous thing that Jesus ever said. With this commandment the Sermon on the Mount reaches its summit. This saying of Jesus has been called 'the capstone of the whole discourse.' It is the topmost peak of social ethics, and the Everest of all ethical teaching."* [53]

We find this teaching in Matthew 7:12: *"So in everything, do to others what you would have them do to you, for this sums up the Law and the Prophets."* It is probable that we should consider these words as a summary of the ethical teaching given by Jesus in His sermon. The word "so" at the beginning of the statement connects it with the other teachings about the correct relationships that we should have with others. Those who belong to the kingdom of God should practice the Golden Rule in all their relationships: in a general sense first, as seen in Matthew 5:7-9, and 33 to 37; then in particular cases, with the brethren in Matthew 5:21-26; and especially in dealing with enemies, in Matthew 5:38-48. In the Golden Rule Jesus orders us to give, to offer, to give extravagantly, the same kind of treatment that we would desire that others give to us.

It is noteworthy that Jesus said that the Golden Rule "sums up the Law and the Prophets." In other words,

---

[53] Barclay, p. 144.

a person who takes this attitude toward his fellow men is fulfilling all the demands of the law given by Moses, given to guide the life of the people, as well as all the teachings of the prophets of God. This is, without doubt, a supreme declaration of Jesus. First, we see His ability to summarize in a short statement all the demands of the law and the prophets. Also, it is shown that faith is an eminently practical matter. Beyond all ceremonies and rituals, faith is revealed and becomes incarnate in my relationship with others. My faith becomes tangible in my treatment of my fellow beings.

A faith which cannot produce evidence for its existence is of little or no value. It would be a faith that no one can see, one that cannot be discerned in one's manner of speech, or behavior, or in humble, kind and respectful treatment of others. I should not affirm that my faith is with God only. A close relationship with God affects one's character and all his relationships. Likewise, if I am at fault in human relationships, I will also be at fault with God. Let us recall some of Jesus' teachings given in the same sermon:

"Therefore, if you are offering your gift at the altar and there remember that your brother has something against you, leave your gift there in front of the altar. First go and be reconciled to your brother; then come and offer your gift."[54]

"But I tell you: Love your enemies and pray for those who persecute you, that you may be sons of your Father in heaven.[55]

"For if you forgive men when they sin against you, your heavenly Father will also forgive you. But if you do not forgive men their sins, your Father will not forgive

---

[54] Matthew 5:23-24
[55] Ibid, 5:44-45.

your sins." [56]

The book of Matthew mentions two other occasions when Jesus uses the expression "the law and the prophets." The first is at the beginning of the Sermon on the Mount, when He said, "Do not think that I have come to abolish the law or the prophets; I have not come to abolish them but to fulfill them" (Matthew 5:17). Jesus is our great Teacher and example. He came to fulfill the law and the prophets; and in doing so, He gave us an example to imitate.

The apostle Peter, remembering the example of Jesus, wrote in his first epistle: "To this you were called, because Christ suffered for you, leaving you an example, that you should follow in his steps. 'He committed no sin, and no deceit was found in his mouth.' When they hurled their insults at him, he did not retaliate; when he suffered, he made no threats. Instead, he entrusted himself to him who judges justly" (1 Peter 2:21-23). In fulfillment of the law and the prophets, He showed love to His enemies.

The second time that Jesus uses the expression "the law and the prophets" in Matthew is found in chapter 22:40. Jesus answered the question about which commandment of the law is most important by saying that it is to love God with all one's heart and soul, and that the second command is very similar: to love one's neighbor as oneself. He concludes by saying, "All the law and the prophets hang on these two commandments." Loving God as our highest priority will lead us also to love our neighbor. And to love my neighbor as myself means that I give him the best treatment that I can possibly give. By doing so I will fulfill all the demands of the law and the

---

[56] Ibid, 6:14-15.

prophets.

As can been seen here, the Golden Rule is the very essence of the doctrine of the Kingdom. That essence is love. The God who is behind the law and the prophets is love. It is by the love of the Father, channeled through the Son, that we are redeemed on the cross. The Golden Rule summarizes what Jesus expects from each one of His followers, that we love one another as He has loved us. When we love one another we show that we know the God of love, that we have been reached by His Son and filled with the presence of the Holy Spirit. And we cannot say that we love God if we do not love our brother, because the Scripture says, "And he has given us this command: Whoever loves God must also love his brother."[57]

Although the principle of the Golden Rule appears in other religions of the world, there are enormous differences. The love just mentioned is one of them. Another is that Jesus does not present it as a requirement in order to obtain heaven. Rather He presents it as a description of those who are going to heaven. He describes what His followers are like, and how they live, those to whom He promises heaven. Another difference is that this principle is not presented as an ideal to which we dedicate ourselves. It is clear that it is a duty that is a characteristic of His disciples, a lifestyle of those who follow Him. But even more, it is impossible without Him.

What would happen in our home, in our workplace, and in our city if we all practiced the Golden Rule? By

BY PRACTICING THE GOLDEN RULE, WE WILL ATTAIN DIAMOND-QUALITY CONDUCT.

---

[57] 1 John 4:8

126

practicing the Golden Rule, we will attain diamond-quality conduct. And what home does not need it? But how, when, and where should I apply the Golden Rule? The only valid answer must be: in every possible way, in every opportunity that I have, in every place that I can.

How would you like others to treat you when you get home? Please make a list, at least mentally, of the sort of treatment you would wish to receive at home. Perhaps it would include points like: to feel loved; to know that what you do is appreciated; to receive respect and admiration. Would you like to receive words of stimulation and congratulations for your achievements, to hear more of "please" and "thank you"? Surely you would not want to receive insults, slanders, humiliation, abuse, crude or hurtful words. You would not want to be ignored, but rather made to feel comfortable, secure, and at peace in your home. Would these things be on your list? Wonderful!

Please take this list and practice it with each member of your family. This is what the Golden Rule of Jesus is like. It is not only that I do not do bad things that I would not want to receive, but rather that I do the good things that I wish to receive. It is a proactive attitude, leading me to do positive things, not only to avoid negative things.

If there is anyone with whom we should practice the Golden Rule, that person is our spouse. Since our spouse is the center of our home, and the home is the center of society, it is well worthwhile to practice the Golden Rule so that the healing, revitalizing influence that comes from following it may begin to affect our married life. Then continue to apply it in the other relationships of the home (parents and children, brothers and sisters, etc.). Continue doing this until it extends outside the home and affects your relationship with your neighbors, the way you drive your car, even the way in which you treat animals. Can there be any problem that cannot be resolved in the home if the spouses treat each other as they would want to be treated? What if you were to try to discover what pleases your spouse, and try to make that loved one happy?

Please ask yourself questions like these, and see whether you have been breaking the Golden Rule in your marriage relationship:
1. Would I like my spouse to treat me as I have been treating him or her lately?
2. How would I feel if I found out that my "better half" is saying about me the things that I have been saying about him or her?
3. What would happen if my spouse begins to use the same excuses that I am using?
4. How would I feel if my spouse begins to use the same words and the same tone of voice that I have been using lately to talk to him or her?
5. In general, would I want my spouse to imitate my attitudes and behavior?

Ken Sande in his book: *The Peacemaker: A Biblical Guide to Resolving Personal Conflict,* says: *"If you find that you dislike the way your spouse is treating you it's because it has fallen below the standards that Jesus established to rule all human relations. If you acknowledge its emptiness before God and the person you have offended, you can start to move forward along the path of forgiveness, agreement and reconciliation.*[58]
As we have been saying, by following the Golden Rule, we will have diamond-quality conduct, and every one

[58] Sande, K., The Peacemaker: A Biblical Guide to Resolving Personal Conflict, (Billings, MT: Peacemaker Ministries) pp. 147–148.

of us needs it. Take heart, there is still hope for your marriage. Don't give up. Get up, seek God's help, and get to work!

Questions for discussion:

1. The Golden Rule summarizes what Jesus expects from each of us. Is it easy for you to obey this rule?

2. Do you practice the Golden Rule in your marriage? Explain.

3. What would you think if your spouse gave you the same treatment that you give him or her? What would you do to correct things that need to be changed?

4. What would happen in our homes, in our workplaces, and in our city if we all practiced the Golden Rule?

Bibliography

1. Alix, Juan Antonio. Décimas Dominicanas de Ayer y de Hoy. Santo Domingo: Publicaciones América, 1986.

2. Álbun canción y letra. ¿Quién lo va a saber? http://www.albumcancion yletra.com/quien-lo-va-a-saber_ de_lolita-flores_91542.aspx. (Nov. 4, 2013)

3. Aguiló, Alfonso. s/f. Caracter-libertad-compromiso. http://www.interrogantes.net/Caracter-libertad-compromiso/menu-id-22.html. (January 3, 2014)

4. Animal Consciousness. Siren Songs. http://www.concienciaanimal. cl/paginas/ temas/ imprimirtemas.php?d=500. (December 17, 2013)

5. Barclay, William. The Gospel of Matthew. Volume 1. Philadelphia: The Westminster Press, 1975

6. Bible, King James Version. Philadelphia: American Bible Society, 2010.

7. Bible, New International Version. Gran Rapids: Zondervan, 1999.

8. Building a better world. Temperaments.. http://nelmazuera.blogspot com/2010_09_27_ archive.html. (January 12, 2014)

9. Definicion.de. Compromiso. http://definicion.de/compromiso. (October 18, 2013)

10. Eggerichs, Emerson. Love & respect: the love she most desires, the respect he desperately needs Nashville: Thomas Nelson, 2004.

11. El Bufón Digital. Burn the ships. http://elbufondigital.Blogspotcom/ 2008/01/quemar-las-navesquien-fu-el-primero.html. (April 20, 2013)

12. Esteban 2008. Siren songs. http://esteban2008.wordpress.com/2008/02/29/los-cantos-de-sirena/. (December 13, 2013)

13. García, Miguel. The Trojan Horse. http://recuerdosdepandora.com/mitos/el-caballo-de troya. (June 27, 2013)

14. Huffingtonpost.com. http://www.huffingtonpost.com/2008/03/12/spitzers-resignation-spee_n_91157.html (January 2, 2012)

15. FamilyLife. Weekend to Remember: Conference Manual (Litter Rock: Christian Life Incorporated. 2003.

16. Lago, José I. How was Troy? http://www.historialago.com /leg_troy_ 01015_ comoera_01.htm. (June 28, 2013)

17. The New York Times. Jim Bakker. http://www.nytimes.com/1987/03/21/us/bakker-evangelist-resigns-his-minstry-over- sexualincident. html (February 2, 2012).

18. Maxwell John C. Ethics 101: There's Only One Rule for Making Decisions. New York: First Warner Books Printing, 2003.

19. Maxwell, John C. The 17 Essential Qualities of a Team Player. Nashville: Thomas Nelson, Inc., 2002.

20. Nos divorciamos.com. Las alarmantes estadisticas del divorcio. http://www.nosdivorciamos.com/? quien=bW9kdWxvPWludGVybmEmdGFibGE9YXX J0aWN1bG8mb3BjaW9uPTE3. (January 16, 2014)

21. Ortega y Gasset, José. Meditaciones del Quijote. Madrid: Publicaciones de la Residencia de Estudiante, 1914.

22. Paez, Oswaldo. Amar y querer. http://elblogdelbolero.wordpress.com/2008/06/25/ manuel-alejandro-el-compositor-del-amor/ (Octubre 12, 2013).

23. Poemas del alma. I cultive a white rose. http://www.poemas-del-alma.com/jose-marti-cultivo-una-rosa-blanca.html. (January 12, 2013)

24. Poesía.bligoo.com. Achilles' heel. http://poesia.bligoo.com/content/view123488/ Aquiles.html. (June 4, 2013).

25. Record, Bob. Beneath the Surface Nashville: B&H Publishing Group, 2002

26. Rapture ready. The who's who of prophecy. http://www.raptureready.com/ who/Jimmy_ Swaggart.html. (February 6, 2012)

27. Sabiduría.com. Revenge.. http://www.sabidurias.com/result_tag.php?alabr a=venganza&lang=es&tag=1840&_pagi_pg=2. (February 6, 2012)

28. Sánchez, Carlos Cuauhtémoc. Código de honor (Code of honor) Audio book. Chicago: Giron Books, 2004.
29. Sande, K., The Peacemaker: A Biblical Guide to Resolving Personal Conflict. Billings, MT: Peacemaker Ministries

30. Temperaments.http://www.slideshare.netbjoven central /temperamentos-4676006?nomobile=true (January 12, 2014).

31. Ultraguia. Burn the ships. www.ultraguia.com.ar. Quemar las naves. www.ultraguia.com.ar//Ultra Sociales/ParaPensar/ParaPensar09.html) (April 20, 2013).

32. Wikipedia. Achilles' Heel. http://es.wikipedia.org/wiki/ Talón_de_Aquiles.(Julio 12, 2013).

33. Wikipedia. Burn the ships. http://es.wikipedia.org/ wiki/Quemar_las_naves. (Abril 21, 2013)

34. Wikipedia. Revenge. http://es.wikipedia.org/wiki/ Venganza (January 15, 2013).

35. Wikipedia. Sirens. http://es.wikipedia.org/wiki/ Sirena. (September 4, 2013).